THE ETERNAL DESTINY SERIES
BOOK ONE

So Shall It Forever Be

THE MAKING OF SATAN

CHRIS & GUY
PAGANO

INKS &
BINDINGS

Inks and Bindings
888-290-5218
www.inksandbindings.com
orders@inksandbindings.com

CONTENTS

To my wife, Alyce, and my three precious
children, Hannah, Guy, and Duncan

ACKNOWLEDGEMENT

I want to acknowledge my family for helping so much in finishing this work. Thank you to my wife, Alyce and my three kids, Hannah, Guy, and Duncan.

When we were younger, I "had" to keep writing and reading this story so the kids could enjoy it as our bedtime story. "Read it again, Daddy." After I finished reading the passages to them, "That was good, Daddy." Many times they were the inspiration and motivation to actually finish what I began in this work. Without them, I am sure this story would never have been finished or published.

Thank you. I love you.

CHAPTER ONE

All the citizens of heaven were excited once the proclamation was made. Everywhere any of the angels went or turned, there was a message about the upcoming award ceremony. As expansive as the kingdom of heaven was, there was no place anybody in it could go without learning of the decree. One of their own members, Lucifer, was going to be anointed as chief over them all. *Why wouldn't he be chosen?* All others agreed. After all, the messenger Boston commented, he was the most glorious being in all of creation—except, of course, for God. An excited associate added, "Lucifer is the largest, most intelligent, fastest, and brightest of all the creatures of light." Having lived and served so long with him, Oslo, Berlin, London, and San Juan admitted that these were "undisputed facts."

Many had seen this anointment coming and thought it was long overdue. "He truly is deserving and worthy," said Boston. "Not only that. Since God Himself issued the decree, there can be no doubt in anybody's mind that, when the title is officially given to Lucifer, it will remain with him for eternity."

Lucifer was, in his own words, magnificent.

No one, except God and Lucifer himself, knew how the grand event would unfold. Both of them had discussed this plan thoroughly and on many occasions.

During the ceremony, each angel expected the grandest of all cherubs to be officially seated above all the other angels and at the right hand of the Almighty. To be sure, it was the highest promotion possible for the angel of light.

As for God Himself, He was not concerned if some would think Him as reduced in status by having a created being at His immediate side. All angels knew from the moment of their creation of the magnanimous nature of this omnipotent King. Many times during their lives, He showed where He considered His own grandeur nothing to be grasped. Actually, He delighted in sharing His glory with His lesser creatures and freely gave to all from His goodness. His joy was to bless others, and in so doing, He hoped to receive the one thing He longed for—reciprocated love.

It was going to be a grand celebration. The Almighty Creator stopped short of nothing in lavishing His splendor on the newly chosen recipient of His divine favor. The largest banquet hall was lined with row after row of the best chairs. As far as the eye could see, there were comfortable places to sit, beautiful carvings, the finest dining ware, and heralding banners. If finances were ever a consideration for one so rich, after looking at all the decor, you might say He spared no expense. For the One who is greater than all of creation, seen and unseen, known and unknown, wealth and riches were merely tokens. The angel, Madrid, was in charge of the hall and was overwhelmed by all the preparations.

As the attendance continued to increase, the invited friends of the angel of honor watched in awe. Berlin and Oslo said they could sense all things spiraling up toward the climax of the evening, when Lucifer would step to the podium to accept this honor and his elevated status. They were so happy for their friend.

The music continued to play. Merriment was in the air. Every one of the heavenly dignitaries were present for the occasion and took their seats. Olympus and Elmira spoke praise of the vaunted celebrant in whose honor they had assembled.

Finally, the Almighty Himself took the podium. God spoke of His pleasure and delight to be able to bestow this award on one so faithful and hardworking. God really had a way of holding the attention of His audience. Each angel in the kingdom hung on every word as He eloquently verbalized on the exquisite virtues of His friend Lucifer. He was very interesting. His timing was perfect. As He spun His discourse on the attributes of Lucifer, it became more and more apparent to all who watched and listened that the only true beauty and splendor resided in the One who held the podium.

As God went on, even the one He talked about became diminished in his own eyes through comparison. This realization increasingly grew on Lucifer, and he became angry. He privately hated the Good One for that.

Finally, the Lord turned His gaze from the audience and to the one He spoke of. He held out His hand and the audience clapped raucously as the Creator called Lucifer to the podium.

Slowly, Lucifer arose and approached the microphone. He wasn't as confident as he had been before. As the two stood together on the stage, the many angels whispered to each other about their observations. London saw what they all felt to be true but now was nakedly obvious. The only true beauty belonged to God.

As this silent drama continued, Lucifer sensed the audience's disappointment in him. He felt sure that he was the source of their dissatisfaction. He turned to face the assembly. The smiles on so many of their faces had turned to blank stares, and Lucifer felt it was all God's fault. *Why did He have to stand up here so long before finally introducing me?* he thought. Lucifer felt offended; the longer he thought about it, the more his anger was fueled. Once this was over and his power was installed, Boston would later overhear him say, "I'm gonna get old Jehovah back for this."

Now it was his turn to speak. Lucifer had waited for this moment for a long time. For eons, he had believed himself worthy of all glory and honor bestowed in heaven. He never considered that up until then his fellow angels didn't considered anyone, even him, to be equal to their Maker. One thing Lucifer failed to realize through all his life was that those in the audience already knew the only One he was describing, as he spoke so glowingly, and it wasn't him.

Many times a peculiar thing happens to those who address audiences. Inevitably, gradually, they become increasingly aware of their listeners' opinions of them while they speak. As the speech continues, the orator feels his or her listeners' feelings and senses the impact of his or her presentation upon them. If things happen to be going well, this feedback can provide an uplifting spirit to the speaker. Unfortunately for Lucifer, this was not the case. The lack of energy in the room failed to elicit the feeling of glory he had been hoping to bask in.

As the honoree continued to speak, he felt a sinking sensation beginning to gnaw at his stomach. Many in the audience was beginning to fidget, even struggling to remain cordial and polite. There was no way they could mentally ascend to the heights that Lucifer described for himself.

San Juan and Madrid looked at each other in disbelief. "How is he going to be the one to usher a new more glorious era into the kingdom?" Madrid commented to his friend.

Perhaps if one of the cherubs or simply an angel had presented the podium to Lucifer, his speech would not have been so anticlimactic. Since God was on the scene, actually on the same stage with him, Lucifer did not appear to fare well.

As Lucifer spoke, it felt to the listeners more like he droned on and on. "Every day I lead us to greatness in worship. Since I was installed as lead singer, the music has never sounded better." He continued, "I have made this kingdom so much more beautiful. My leadership will only continue to improve heavenly life for everybody."

Was he ever going to end this self-congratulatory monologue? His speech was the precursor to future dictators' orations, which would go on and on for hours, serving no purpose but to control their subjects and keep them uncomfortable.

Finally, he concluded his self-adulating remarks and everybody burst out of the auditorium and into the hallways, like those escaping a fire in a room where the oxygen had been depleted.

It wasn't long until the comments about "the speech" began.

Most had seen Lucifer's true nature for the first time. Those were the ones who would remain forever loyal to the Holy One. As they talked about the recent celebration, it became clear to them how this whole turn of events had taken place. To no one's surprise, as Lucifer spoke, his words had produced the effect of minimizing himself and magnifying God. This was by no means what he had intended to do. "Lucifer should have been appreciative and grateful," said the assistant worship leader. "That is what he was supposed to do."

Without a dispute, God won the hearts of many through loving his nemesis when He could have ignored or destroyed him instead. In effect, however, Lucifer was seen by most for who and what he was, a wanna be.

"The award was enough," commented London. "Why did he have to go and speak so highly of himself?"

Most in attendance no longer held Lucifer in high esteem. Lucifer's actions and attitude were such an affront to them that it altered their assessment of him. They no longer regarded him as anything special. He was merely a created being, just like all of them except bigger and a better musician, they commented.

Remarkably, there was a group, about a third of the assembly, who actually favored Lucifer even more after his rambling rampage. As these "fans of Lucifer" discussed the recent forum, they glowed with admiration. Many of the fans agreed that they were quite impressed by Lucifer's beauty, his immense size, his luminous aura, and the way he could spin information to his advantage. He was quite impressive, in deed, Lynch commented. How had he become so wonderful?

CHAPTER TWO

Lucifer dispatched Merchury as messenger to secretly get the word out. All those willing to support Lucifer and aid him in acquiring more power were to meet for an important planning session. Once all the angels who loved Lucifer had reassembled, Dis and Condone began to clamor for him. The crowd of admiring cherubim joined in. All present sensed that they had been given a golden opportunity to gain status, and they weren't going to let it slip away. Chorazin and Decapo deduced that, if they just pushed and prodded their champion to seize greater control, then they too could advance by clinging to his coattails.

"Why don't we push ahead with a plan for you to become king?" Pride shouted.

They soon found out that Lucifer needed no prodding or inducements to do anything that might elevate him further. He yelled back that he had already planned to ascend to the place of God, with or without their help.

The din of conversation steadily grew as they all agreed that the promotion did not go far enough. Scoundrel yelled from the back exaltedly, "Lucifer is worthy to sit on high. He should sit on the gates of the dawn. Let the Most High make room for him for all to behold."

These comments soon became chants. And soon after, the gathering had developed into a movement intended to force Lucifer's coronation right now.

Crepe was the first one at Lucifer's side asking for an

assignment to get this plan initiated.

Upon hearing Crepe's request, Complicit expressed anger about Crepe trying to "steal Lucifer's thunder." He too wanted the job.

A few angels who were not involved with this secrecy were nearby, close enough to hear the confusion, and went to see what all the commotion was about. To their horror, Gains and Olympus quickly understood that what they were witnessing was treason. Gains yelled to Olympus, "This pitiful band of malcontents is in an uproar at the prospect of dethroning the King."

"We want Lucifer. We want Lucifer! We have no part in the Most High," Condone, Dis, and the rest shouted.

In an attempt at heroism, the two witnesses tried to disband the throng by physically removing them from the action. This worked only temporarily, as the two were then summarily seized upon and expelled by the many from the crowd.

Immediately upon their forced removal, Gains and Olympus sounded the angelic alarm for Ignus, the captain of the guard, to come and intervene in order to put down this collective foolishness. Upon Ignus' command, a host of powerful angels descended on the cadre of anarchists and, by their sheer force of numbers, brought a measure of calm to the assembly.

In spite of this, the battle lines were clearly being drawn, as it became apparent to which camp on this issue each angel belonged. Those who lived for the glory of the Lord were opposed to the other side, which wanted so-called equality for all through Lucifer. The captain, Ignus, and his camp tried desperately and in vain to persuade their old companions to forsake their folly and rejoin their old ranks before it was too late. There were a few who, seeing the error of this nonsense, did indeed recant and rejoin the righteous.

Sadly, however, the majority of the protesters had no intention of turning back and were only emboldened to resist. "We are going to get our due or face the consequences of trying," yelled Ghenghis.

Ignus asked Chorazin and Decapo whether they have given any consideration to the inevitable consequences for carrying this plan to its end.

Both just looked at him, shaking their heads. "Like what?" Decapo asked.

Puzzled by this response, Ignus later said to Gains and Olympus, "Clearly, none of the agitators had any idea of what or how severe the consequences of their decision could be."

Nevertheless everyone agreed to Ignus's request for calm. Secretly, however, the rebels meant to wait for a more opportune time to strike.

There was, indeed, a cessation of hostilities that followed this conflict. And for the majority of the angels who had attempted to prevent this division, the calm was of great comfort. To those faithful servants, the thought of the punishment for treason was beyond conception. "What really is separation, torment, and isolation?" asked Omaha.

As it was in those days, these things simply did not exist within the kingdom of heaven—to say nothing of brimstone, anguish, or gnashing of teeth. Such things had not entered the minds of created beings who could never enforce them upon another.

"Perhaps that was why those unfaithful servants did not fear such an experience as they should have. To them, such things simply are not real enough to contemplate," surmised Ignus.

The peacekeepers departed from the place of the uprising and rested in the fragile assurance that unity had been restored and accepted that Lucifer was now placed above them all as the Holy One ordained for him. "I hope this works out well for us," said Boston.

One-third of their ranks were not righteous or loyal. Crepe

and Complicit were continuing to secretly confer with Lucifer regarding his plans for greater advancement. Many others saw what the two were doing and joined in a growing conference with Lucifer.

Lucifer asked those assembled, "Do you wish for advancement? Do you want more enlightenment? Follow me, and you won't have to answer to the Holy One. You'll become rulers with me. For you, this will be an opportunity to move to a better enlightenment. No longer will you have to answer directly to the Holy One and wait for His directives to complete a task no matter how far beneath you it is."

Merchury, Condone, Assassin, Ghenghis, Angus, and all the others were going to become princes and rulers in the realm of heaven with an autonomy previously unknown.

"Lucifer personally certified this to be true to each one of us who was bold enough to back him, so we know it is true," said Glutton to Sloth.

CHAPTER THREE

Michael said to Gabriel later that he had come to learn that, through this whole drama, the Almighty One had watched each one's every move, although He was not physically present. From His throne, He beheld all the underlings as they debated and battled for prevalence and peace, supremacy and order. In His gaze, He not only saw but he also heard their actions, words, and activities. He also saw the unseen entities of intent, motivation, aspiration, and the yet unknown reality of evil.

"Soon, though, this masked beast of evil will reveal itself for all to see, emerging from the dark unknown recesses of the heart of Lucifer," God had admitted. "When it is revealed, it will show itself capable of possessing all who agree with him." The ultimate judge had seen what would come but still rested without taking any action. "For now is not the time," He counseled.

"God was sure of its presence. There was no doubting that. He knew the right time and method required to deal with mutiny, and He was not going to be persuaded to act before the time was right," Gabriel continued. "He knows the end from the beginning—he did even before there was such a thing as 'the beginning.' Whether it is all in the plan, or if there was a plan, or if there was going to be a plan, now that this entity has arisen in our midst, none of us can know with certainty," he said.

"This is known only by Him. The answers to those concerns rest in His own mind, possibly never to be revealed to us," agreed Michael.

The disruptive riot with Lucifer and his followers caused many of the faithful to discuss their God in greater detail. Berlin, Oslo, London, Rome, Rio, and Omaha sat together to try to understand what the rebels' grievance was. Their thoughts turned to the Holy One. "He is a being beyond description," Rome said, speaking for them all. "He was not created and has no beginning like all of us. He cannot be overcome or resisted. Exactly what He is does not fit into any categorical definition or description that we can hope to imagine. He is not an angel. Neither is he a cherub or a seraph. Although we resemble Him in many ways and feel as if He has resemblance to us, He is far above us. His majesty is exceedingly beyond ours. We are not created in His image. But He is so personal to each one of us that we often say that we feel that He must be one of us, at least to an extent."

The conversation continued. "He is far above creation yet cannot be separated from what He made. It is as though His whole sense of being is to be found in that relationship. He always delights in His servants the angels and the archangels," Rio said. And at that reflection, his face began beaming with utter joy.

Oslo excitedly interjected, "He obviously loves His creation—the heavens and the great city."

There was, however, to those most closely associated with Him, a subtle sadness or longing. Most of them in the heavenly host did not discern this, but Michael and Gabriel sure did. They often discussed the matter among themselves, with a desire to cure it.

Gabriel said, "I think only God Himself has the depth of understanding of how profound this longing is."

His Spirit grieves at times like one who has lost a son or daughter and hopes to have some of what God described to them as children. But it was not to be. He was very loving and all powerful, and many found this to be quite perplexing.

"How can the one with all power be so concerned about anyone else?" said Michael. "To the exclusion of His own best interests, He helps, blesses, and promotes the welfare of others. It is as if He must express His love more than He expresses His power."

The others agreed, though they didn't understand it completely. Only a few angel's closest to Him knew that, unless or until God had children to love—children who had a choice about whether or not to love Him in return, He might never be as fulfilled as they were by just being with Him. The Lord wanted to be known.

Michael asked Gabriel, "Have you noticed when God is talking about children that He closes His eyes, and a big smile spreads across His beaming face?" "Oh yes, it is such a beautiful sight, I rejoice with Him yet I'm not quite sure I understand it," confided Gabriel.

Prior to the coronation, both Michael and Gabriel, along with Lucifer, were always with the Holy One. For eons, they listened to His counsel, felt His heart, and watched Him do all that He had planned and announced that He would do.

"Many of His plans," Lucifer said, "I simply did not understand. Especially the one in particular that is very mysterious to me." "Jehovah seemed to be most animated about a plan concerning a lamb that was to be slain," he said. "Sometime before the foundation of the earth was laid, there was a lamb that was slain." Jehovah talked about it often with them, but they never grasped what He meant.

"Okay, wait. He was slain and will be slain?" Lucifer would ask. The whole thing was just such a mystery.

God would beam with joy as He thought within Himself concerning this idea and then discussed it with the three archangels along with the many enigmas surrounding it.

"What lamb? And the earth, what is that? What does He mean when He says to slay the lamb? Everybody in heaven knew what lambs are and that they were harmless and lovable creatures. To slay one didn't make sense. Certainly, He must mean something other than what we think it does," Lucifer finished.

Whatever it was and the details concerning that great plan, Michael and Gabriel agreed, it had to be magnificent and grand. In spite of their lack of understanding when it came to some of His ideas, Gabriel, Michael, and Lucifer were all good servants—up until the day of the coronation. On that day and during the ceremony, deceit, lies, and treason would be found in Lucifer. This would have to be dealt with. But in the meantime, God just continued to watch.

All three of them were glorious beings, full of splendor—not in comparison to the Most Holy One, but in comparison to the other created beings. They were large, powerful, intelligent, and capable of completing any task given to them, Lucifer even more so than Michael and Gabriel. Perhaps that was why it was he (and not the other two archangels) who was contemplating the notion of himself as God's rival.

Being equal to God. Lucifer long continued to dwell on that. *After I am someday promoted to chief angel, all the others will grasp the verity of that idea*, he told himself. *They will believe it to be true as if their lives depended on it.* To him, the issue was not the reality of his vision but, instead, getting others to agree with it.

CHAPTER FOUR

Lucifer was quite pleased with the outcome of his last conference. He explained to Ghenghis and Angus, "In one camp are those who remain loyal to the King, and in the other camp are those who are behind me seeking to replace the King."

The angels in both camps frequently discussed the change in Lucifer since the day of his coronation. All those who had sided with him at the beginning secretly pledged their support behind him.

"I am not ready to put myself on the line for him," said Lynch, "but if he keeps convincing me, it won`t be long until I would defiantly follow him anywhere, even right up to the throne of God Himself." The malcontents came up with a plan to enact their agenda and after much deliberation they decided to pursue its ends.

Lucifer and his followers were going to keep making disturbances until it was time to issue a challenge. After this plan was disclosed in detail to every one of the traitors , Lynch and the others who were hesitant to get completely involved decided there was no stopping them now. They were also all together in their willingness to deal with the consequences of enacting the plan—in the unlikely event that they are unsuccessful. "Most likely, we will be enjoying the fruits of success," the crowd clamored.

"If we can successfully depose the Lord and enthrone me, you will rule all of creation," Lucifer bellowed.

There was great risk associated with this plan, for they knew that the loyal ones would fight to the end to save their King. If God Himself got involved in the conflict too soon, their plans would surely fail, and they would face certain doom. "So far, though," Angus said, "He has done nothing." In spite of all the risk, each one at the conference pledged to act as one and go forth with their scheme.

The loyal ones outnumbered the traitors two to one. They continued to notice the difference in Lucifer ever since that award ceremony. Ever since that day when he was placed in authority over them, they all had the unfortunate experience of getting more exposure to him than they had previously. Lucifer delighted in showing off his new status and often reminded all the "underlings" he was dealing with that they were beneath him.

Gains told Moscow he'd heard Lucifer say to a fellow angel, "I am the chosen one, and if the Creator ever got anything right, He sure got that decision right on target. Out of all the reasons the Almighty is worthy of praise from you, the ultimate reason to praise Him is for being smart enough to pick me for this elevated position yet He did not go far enough."

Moscow noted that, as Lucifer's attitude continued to fester, it eventually consumed him. "He has become very shortsighted by his lust for power and ambition for more adoration," he replied. Nothing pleased Lucifer more than to watch the underlings react in haste to any order he bellowed upon them.

Does God even know what's going on? many of His subjects wondered. *Is all of this happening with His approval?*

Omaha and Rio commented, "This whole thing is beginning to turn in a bad way." Gains agreed with the complainers. "The longer it goes on, the worse it's getting."

Olympus agreed. "With Lucifer in charge now, the situation is abusive to everyone." Moscow remarked, "He is disrespectful of God and all the good things that He has done for him."

Increasingly, Lucifer and his minions were separating themselves from the others as if they were a corps or a battalion. As this divide continued to widen, they gradually developed a gang-like mentality and identity. Crypt and Bloodd were very animated and devised hand gestures and signals peculiar to their group. Try as they all did to conceal their opposition to the establishment, it was becoming increasingly obvious—to the point that even the most stationary and uninvolved sentry could see the changes. Things that had never taken place in the open before now occurred regularly and brazenly.

"How did they ever imagine that they could conceal their changes from the One that knows all?" said Oslo.

"Do they even care anymore?" replied Madrid.

Differences in affiliations, associations, attitudes, speech and attendance patterns, verbal expression, and even slight physical changes in appearance had all become evident as the handiwork of Crypt and Bloodd.

"Perhaps they don't care if He knows," Oslo agreed. "Or maybe they just deceived themselves into believing that He would not notice or take concern."

The tension is getting really out of hand, thought Michael. *Maybe He is afraid to confront Lucifer and his band or is even one of them.* "No! That can't be it," he chided himself for those thoughts.

Like an oncoming storm on a humid summer evening, the dark ominous clouds of violence and uncertainty were on the not so distant horizon.

As the Lord of Hosts continued to love all of His created servants the loyal ones were left to wonder just what was going on in the kingdom. "It has come to the point where He is being subtly yet openly ridiculed," Boston said.

"If that continued to happen, He will surely act," his friends continued to believe.

Gabriel privately told Michael, "He must put a stop to this uneasiness, the division, the disrespect and mockery, and the looming threat of chaos or mutiny."

CHAPTER FIVE

It was reported by Boston that the Lord was conferring with Himself—the Creator, the Eternal Word, and the Holy Spirit. This was a good sign for the loyal ranks, and all who heard the news became greatly encouraged. Whenever this occurred, something huge and wonderful shortly followed.

After the last time it was known to have happened, the Word began being addressed under a new title—as "the Son" and also "the Lamb." The Creator was known also as the Father. No one knew why the Creator and the Spirit called the Word Son and Lamb from the point of that meeting onward and the Creator was called Father. Most figured it had something to do with the planning that had taken place during their conference. It was surely a mystery that many of the angels longed to look into but couldn't. The loyal angels esteemed the Creator's wisdom and plans as too wonderful to comprehend.

Nevertheless, they all knew what one of the main topics of discussion was sure to be at this conference—Lucifer and his growing band of challengers and their gross disrespect.

"It all could have been put down by Him so easily if only He would do what I would do and do it now," said Imp.

Michael chastised him for making that comment, and Imp would decide later to join the traitors because of it. "He simply does not work as we do and His plans are magnificent," Michael told him. "So whatever He is going to do is going to be awesome."

Imp remain unconvinced and unconcerned.

Following any of the great God's conference, a proclamation

would always be issued. The Lord would dispatch Boston and his aids as messengers to all corners of the kingdom to bring the news.

In this case, the directive was that every individual was to attend a very large assembly. It was to be attended by all, without exception. The Almighty God was going to be there and attend to the pressing matter of what to do with disunity in the kingdom once and for all.

Off in the distant recesses of the kingdom Lucifer was playing music for the smaller army of subjects who now followed him when they received the summons to attend a gathering before the Lord with all the citizens of the kingdom. The archangel became immediately incensed by the unannounced interruption. "Who do you think you are interrupting me?" he bellowed at the courier.

The messengers had known they had to inform Lucifer and his followers, "for they still reside in the kingdom and are citizens," Boston reminded them.

"It might be their opinion that this status of citizen is merely a technicality," one of the messengers had surmised. "Their words Godward are praiseworthy, but their hearts and deeds seemed to be far from Him. It appears that they had, at some point, all but renounced their heavenly citizenship," replied Valor.

"Who would deliver the message to him?" Boston and his aids had debated together.

Finally, Valor had decided to accept the assignment. And now, as he brought the message, he was not surprised at Lucifer's reception. "A change needs to occur if you are going to stay here," was Valor's response to Lucifer. Then he hurriedly got out of there before being apprehended.

"Where could we go if we have to leave?" the summoned ones asked. "A new place would have to be built, and they did not know how to do that." They all contemplated this prospect—a new place, a new kingdom.

Lucifer stated that he had no intention of leaving. "I am not going anywhere."

If I get things to go my way, he stated, *God will be the one getting evicted from the kingdom.* "God", he went on, "was the one who would be thrown down and removed. No one would ever be hearing from ol' Jehovah and His pitiful band of friends ever again."

"God might have an agenda for this upcoming assembly. But He will soon find out that my agenda will prevail. *He* will be asking *me* for mercy and direction to His new domicile," Lucifer told his band, and he thoroughly enjoyed their laughter at his disrespect.

This was the time and place where Lucifer was going to spring his trap and launch his plan. "The one who used to rule," as Lucifer now called God, might have an agenda for the meeting. But that was going to change once I arrive. My plan is to upstage God this time in grand fashion. During the last convocation, I had been way too passive. I'd only received what had been given to me. I had not shone as brightly as I know Icould." *This time things are going to be different.* "I am going to seize the moment, force the opportunity, dictate the agenda, and secure an outcome suitable for a new king," swore Lucifer.

CHAPTER SIX

The time had come. The Grand Reception Hall was prepared and filling up fast. Everybody was there or soon to be. In a few moments, the Speaker would begin, once all had a chance to sit down. "Strangely, there is one person not here yet," Crepe noted. "All are present except Lucifer." "This is the moment he has been waiting for—the right time, the right place, the right atmosphere, the right reason. Everything seems to be in his favor," he quietly uttered.

The hall quickly filled. "There is no empty seat to be found," Madrid stated, "God knows how many chairs He needed, for He knows how many angels He created. He knows each one intimately—their names, faces, spirits, sizes, and shapes." God had instructed him beforehand on the number of seats needed. "Why was there one chair without someone in it?" he mused.

That was plain for all to see, because that empty seat was up front on the stage next to the Most High's seat. They all saw it, but none made any comment due to the uncertainty of the tenuous situation.

The gavel sounded. All chatter and background noises ceased as all eyes turned toward the front of the hall to where the podium was. The announcement was made. The Holy One was just then entering the room and striding to the lectern.

At that moment, Lucifer also burst into the room with quite a clamor. Both doors of the double door entrance slammed forcefully against the walls as they ran out of room to keep swinging wider. His entrance seemed to be a little clumsy at first.

Most noticed a hard, defiant look in his eyes, while his mouth was spewing boastfully.

To the astonishment of all who had gathered, Lucifer was apparently challenging the Ancient of Days. In front of everybody in the kingdom, Lucifer asserted himself and attempted to supplant God and insert himself in His place as Supreme Head over all.

"The kingdom now belongs to me," Lucifer roared across the room. "From now on, everybody will look at me as the source of all their pleasures. The old King is now relieved of His duties."

He then turned to face God Almighty and said, "You may leave now. Your services are no longer required within this kingdom." He then threatened the Ancient of Days. "Since You claim to be wise, You should take this opportunity I'm giving You to vacate on Your own, because help will be given if You resist. I have more than enough help here—help from seasoned and personally trained warriors—to aid me in Your removal, if that is required."

"How can this be?' asked Austin. "This is utterly bewildering."

Everyone who had gathered went ice-cold as the drama gained momentum. The only thing that could be heard was the piercing sound of Michael and Gabriel pulling their swords from their scabbards. But the Lord prevented it.

It was one of those rare moments where you see what is going on before your very eyes yet have no way of comprehending what is happening because it is unprecedented. Everyone stared in stunned disbelief—even those backing Lucifer.

Complicit and Decapo were taken by total surprise at this. They had expected to be more involved when the plan is put into action, not knowing that Lucifer considered them all clumsy accomplices, incapable of rising to this occasion. "No," he yelled at them. "I got this myself."

This was something Lucifer was sure of—he would do better without their "help." "Just me and Jehovah, me and You!" he yelled.

God was aware that Lucifer had never understood that he too was a created being with limitations. He was not without a beginning. Nor was he omniscient or omnipotent like God was.

San Juan and Damascus spoke quietly together. The audacity of this action was so foolhardy, so impossible. "This must be a staged stunt with God and Lucifer working cooperatively to make a point," San Juan concluded. "No one can challenge the Almighty," Damascus agreed. "No one!"

As the standoff continued for what seemed like eons, many in the assembly considered together these facts: They knew that God had summoned the entire population here to discuss or do something about the "Lucifer issue." Was this it? Had He and Lucifer reconciled and the two devised this drama as an act to demonstrate an important point? Many on both sides of the aisle thought this was the case.

Yet there he was, and his efforts were picking up a rhythm, gaining coordination and momentum. Still the Lord let him rant and rave, not silencing him even as Lucifer's hoards began to get agitated.

Lucifer spoke more boastfully. "You just continue to sit there? Rise up off Your throne for one last time, and either come to me to receive Your just due or just keep walking out the door. See I made it easy for You. Both doors are swinging wide open after my entrance."

He continued, "I have come to take my rightful place. I will ascend to the highest heaven. I will seat myself above the Morning Star. I will rule the kingdom. I will be the object of affection, and I will be the foundation upon which all things are built. I will be the first, and I will be the last. All preeminence will be in me. From now on, anyone who does not salute me with praise will be punished. But since I am kind and benevolent, I will show mercy at some point. I will make this kingdom great. All will know that I am what I am!"

Now that the treasonous band knew exactly what Lucifer's plan was, they sat motionless, stunned by this blatant, leaping grab for power. Dis whispered to Lynch, "Is it going to work?" They were uncertain that this was the way they wanted to get jettisoned into power.

Silence fell throughout all of heaven for a time.

Lucifer was at the forefront, standing in front of the King he had so brazenly challenged, awaiting a reaction.

Ignus asked Michael, "What will He do about this? Will He need a supporting cast, an army of loyalists or anybody?"

"The Lord said to stand down," Michael replied.

Finally, the One True God began to cause a separation in the crowd. As a shepherd separates the sheep from the goats, He put each angel in one group or the other—two on the right, one on the left, two on the right, one the left.

In the end, everyone in attendance was put in one camp or the other—everyone, that is, except Lucifer. He was alone now with no group looking so eager to back him. Amazingly, all those loyal to righteousness were on the right and the treasonous ones were put on the left. Fear fell upon all those on the left like a mighty cascading waterfall.

Michael and Gabriel knew that God was ready to act. The time to move had come, and He was going to do something definitive and climactic.

With a Word and a gesture of His mighty right hand, the Everlasting God bound Lucifer. Seven unbreakable bands held him fast, and squirm as he did, he was not going to get free. One band covered his eyes. Another bound his boastful mouth. One held his shoulders, and another was around his arms at the elbows. One held his hands at his waist, one was around his knees, and the last band was around his ankles. Wrapped tightly around him, each band was made of an unknown, indestructible product. The bands had come from the mouth of the Word, now called the Son and the Lamb.

"See, I told you. Just have faith in Him. It will be all right," Michael said to Ignus.

Now Lucifer was the focus of everybody's attention. Somehow this was just not the way he'd planned on getting that to happen. Everyone stared at him—some with victorious expressions, others in dread, depending on what side they were on. "Oh no," whispered Drakon, "this does not look good for us." Lucifer stood there, bound and silent. Some thought he would successfully break loose, but he was powerless against the Word of the Lord.

As he continued his struggles, he became quite comical and amusing, prompting muffled giggles from the faithful ones, who were trying not to laugh. "But he was so funny. I couldn't help it," Gains later said to the others in defense of his actions. They also finally acknowledged that they had done it too.

Once that scene grew tiresome, all eyes turned toward the group on the left. What would they do now? This was the commonly whispered question.

Ignus and Gabriel were sure. "There is no turning back for those scalawags," said Gabriel.

"I tried to warn them of the consequences of treason," Ignus replied, his tone emphasizing his frustration with Lucifer's band.

The followers of Lucifer had already crossed the line of no return some time ago. It was too late for them.

As they stared fearfully at Him who was forever true, they knew their just conviction was imminent and their sentence soon to follow.

Another Word and a wave of His righteous right hand, and Michael and Gabriel sprang into action. Out came the swords again, and the loyal ones each grabbed a traitor two on one, until all were arrested. One shackling band was spoken upon each of them by the Word as well, so they were no longer free to move about at all.

With all the citizens of heaven in attendance, the grand trial was about to begin. Each and every traitor was going to stand before the Righteous Judge for treasonous deeds. Not a single word would be uttered from any of them throughout the course of the long proceeding concerning the charges brought against them. They were all without excuse. Only the cries and whimpering from those not strong enough to face their fate silently were heard.

Michael tapped the gavel and pointed toward a visual display that had just appeared above them. There, before the eyes of all present in the vast assembly, every word, deed, and thought the defendants had ever said, done, or had was put on public display. As if watching a video, the Judge and His friends watched the guilt of the guilty trail through the ethosphere for all to view, and none of it could be brought back for another try. It was too late for them.

One by one, the guilty were lead to a holding cell to be detained there until the last scoundrel received his due verdict and was put there with the others. From there, their next destination was going to be someplace awful. A new place of confinement had been established for all of them. The details of that place were still a little sketchy, but the prison guards Tokyo and Istanbul had let word get out that the Righteous Judge had big plans for that place and for the guilty.

The last one to stand before the Judge was Lucifer. For that event, every angel, cherub, seraphim, and archangel was especially interested in watching. Even the ones who had already been confined were given remote access via the ethosphere for them to watch the spectacle and to see him get served his fate.

The video display of Lucifer's crimes was quite appalling

to all who watched and heard. None were aware that he had been working so feverishly in secret to accomplish his objective, overthrowing the throne. They had no idea that God had, in fact, known it all along and in every detail. He had kept it to Himself until the Day of Judgment, which was reserved for all those who rebelled.

Like all the others, Lucifer had no response regarding his charges, being abundantly convinced of his guilt. He did request permission to speak regarding another matter. All condemned prisoners are granted final words if they choose to speak. Perhaps that custom arose from the trial of Lucifer.

The gracious Lord instructed the captains to remove the band that was upon Lucifer's mouth. What came out shortly after they had done so had never been heard before. No one expected to hear such vile filth from this ex-director of heavenly worship. What followed was pure vileness and putrefaction full of slime and debauchery. All who heard it could not understand why God let him continue to speak at all, since all he did was slander the one who had judged him.

Lucifer began, "You say that you are a glorious God. You claim to be magnanimous and full of grace. How long did we have to endure those sycophants drooling over you? You might be powerful, but you know nothing of righteousness, only judgment and finding fault. You know nothing of mercy and especially nothing about love. You should never say any other rambling phrase about Your love or some such nonsense of You being Love. No one within the sound of my voice sees or has ever seen this love in You that You love to boast of. If it did exist in You, it wouldn't be real but only a setup to get something that you want from all of us. You are a sham, and I am here only because I exposed You for what You are, and You don't like it. You are a fraud Who speaks of love and uses it as a weapon against Your enemies and as a tool to serve Yourself among your friends. Go ahead, "most loving one," and ship me out of here. But remember this: My words will never be forgotten although I am gone."

The Word of God placed the band over Lucifer's mouth again and read the verdict. Next came the pronouncement that shook heaven with violent tremors. With all eyes watching and every heart beating like the pounding of a million hooves, the angel Bailiff read the verdict and proclaimed out loud, "Lucifer, regarding the charge of treasonous perfidy, you have been found—*guilty*."

Everybody heard those words, for there was no mistaking them. As a result of watching the drama that had unfolded, no one considered the decision unjust. Lucifer's guilt was plainly evident and put in a showcase that confirmed their thoughts, as they had all experienced his evil deeds.

New Delhi said to Rome, "Did you think He would do anything other than what was right?" The only issue that had not been resolved until then was whether the Righteous One would bring justice or overlook all offences through favoritism. That was just something that He could not do. "See, I told you," New Delhi added, following up his question with the answer to his own question. "He is forever true and never changing. He could not deny who He is."

Bailiff bellowed again, "Lucifer and his hoard are to be expelled from heaven and caused to fall to a lower region in the creation previously unknown to all but held in the mind of the Great God. To that place, you are all to be banished."

Out from behind the judge's desk came two very large, very powerful cherubim, who snatched up Lucifer and brought him to a place where, at that very moment, a growing fissure opened up in the floor of the hall. And then the silent Lucifer was pushed through the gaping chasm, along with all the condemned bound angels of darkness. He was shoved into the hole as if he were a log being thrown onto a bonfire.

Immediately after Lucifer and his followers went through the clearance, the hole closed back up.

A profound and prolonged hush descended upon the witnesses.

Finally, Paris commented, "He was so powerful, so mighty, so proud, and now he is gone."

The scene concluded with a final pronouncement from Bailiff. "So shall it forever be!"

And all of heaven broke out into spontaneous praise of the Righteous King.

CHAPTER SEVEN

I t was considered the end of a glorious era and yet the start of a new one. For sure, this new epoch would come with uncertainty but also with opportunity. For the faithful citizens, it also meant a lot more activity. They would no longer be stationed in heaven alone but would also be in other locations within the soon-to-be expanding creation.

As Lucifer was falling, the Word was watching while He was in the act of creating a new place to contain him. The new location had a resemblance to what would later become known as a planet. Subsequently, it was given the name *earth*. It was a swirling mass of cosmic dust, particulate matter, water vapor, and darkness.

Lucifer and his horde all fell simultaneously, and it appeared as quite a spectacle. They remained as spiritual beings and, so, emanated the light in their bodies that was glimmering and shimmering as they fell. The lighted display was finally halted by any eerie darkness once they reached the outer regions of that new place of darkness and torment, their home.

There in that dark, miserable place, Lucifer was released from his bands and given lordship over the entire realm, holding the deed that gave him title to that formless and void place. In the center of that primordial soup, in the very heart of it, was created a place of utter torment. It was designated upon its creation as a place of abject darkness, separation, and agony for all of the fallen angels condemned to suffer there. Some of their ranks were to be left there in chains—forever.

Once they all ended their descent, they were put in their place for their next appointed punishment. Those who were appointed unto the heart of the earth went to be held there, where there was going to be weeping and gnashing of teeth, fire and brimstone, and separation.

Imp cried out to the others who he could not see but who he knew were there with him, "Why did I let you deceive me? I almost got away from your evil desires. If only I had known about this place and what it's like, I would never have turned from Him."

Terrible sounds of groaning echoed constantly in his ears, and then the chains clanged tightly around his hands and feet.

Others were appointed to the outer darkness, where there was going to be some degree of freedom of movement. To them, an uncertain future of roaming and wondering throughout their new realm was just beginning. There would be no light, no music, no friendship, and no purpose. They would just go from one location to another in one direction or another until they felt like changing that. But they could never leave that place.

The remaining angels who are forever true to the Way, the Truth, and the Life stared in astonishment. In what seemed to be a mere instant, their comrades of eons were discovered, tried, judged, condemned, sentenced, bound, and dispatched away from the Holy One. Out they went, in the blink of an eye, never to be together with Him or anyone again. Out in the distant recesses of the added-on creation, they went—to the outer darkness.

"It all happened so fast," Olympus commented. "It seemed to most of us at the time that God did not ever even know what the guilty departed were doing or maybe didn't care. Then suddenly, all that changed, and the entire situation was dealt with wonderfully. He knew all along. But in gracious kindness, He allowed sin to reach its full measure, in hopes that they would repent before the end. Perhaps they could be salvaged from the ongoing course of actions they took that led to their doom, but it was not to be."

"But they were angelic beings. Certainly there's no redemption for fallen ones who have seen God and resided in His presence," said Rome. "Nevertheless, an interesting attribute in God has been revealed. Imagine," he finished, "God hopes for redemption."

All of those who were left and with the Lord gradually came to the realization that a momentous change had just occurred. It was a change that would affect not only their fellow ex-comrades but them as well and God too.

"Perhaps this is yet another reason He does not jump and pounce on every infringement, infraction, and imperfection as soon as it happens. He knows there will be time for that. The consequences of bringing justice always must be felt by so many, oftentimes bringing unwanted consequences," realized San Juan.

The many loyal ones began to ask questions regarding their relationship with the condemned. "What do we call them?" "What is our interaction with them supposed to be?" "Will we ever see them again?"

Each answer the Supreme Judge gave them generated another series of questions. Truly they were all wrestling with a new reality that went far beyond anything they'd ever thought to be in the realm of possibility.

"One thing was more certain to me," said London. "Through all that just happened, there is no question that God cares for all of us and is sure to deal rightly with every situation when it must be handled."

CHAPTER EIGHT

Down below in the realm of darkness, the fallen ones who could gathered together to confer with Lucifer. Lust, Greed, Sloth, and Envy as they were later called also had questions and hoped that Lucifer would have a plan for future progress.

"What are we going to do to get out of here?" Wrath yelled out in anger. "You were supposed to ascend to the throne, not descend to this pit with all of us. When can we avenge this setback?"

Lucifer took the initiative in response to the continuing line of questions. He was not going to leave the outcome of all of this to some underling to decide. The first order of business on his agenda, Lucifer decided, was to tell them how to address him. "In days past, you all knew me and referred to me by the name given from that deceiver." This was how he now referred to God. "That cold hard thief in heaven gave me the name Lucifer. Therefore, I will no longer answer to that. I have renamed myself Satan. I will not be known by any other name but Lord Satan, and you all need new names as well. There will be no sign of His presence in our realm. This is the land of darkness, with none of His light or so-called life. We are totally separate from them. Have no fellowship with the fruitless deeds of light. If they want to call this death, then let death reign. This is the world of the dead in the land of death, and we are the masters."

Everybody yelled, "Hail, Lord Satan."

At that moment the sound of an eerie wail rose up from beneath them. This was the cry of the spirits being held in the chamber of total darkness in chains. It was a scream of pain, sorrow, torment, and misery. Many of the newly renamed followers took on the collective name of demons. They looked at each other with uncertainty in their eyes. Lucifer decided to command the moment by yelling at the tortured and telling them, "Be quiet down there. We are trying to think."

The demons all got a kick out of Lord Satan.

The laws were being amended in the kingdom of heaven at the same time that they were being enacted in the world below. God Almighty informed His friends that Lucifer and his hoards were banished forever. He explained to them, "Some of you will have to be moved to different posts to do new assignments." He cautioned that they should always be on the watch for any impending encroachment of the enemies, if not an outright attack. "The captains will have to position the sentries and reorganize their ranks. From now on, they must be vigilant to consider the war that they are in and never lose ground to the enemy."

The Mighty Judge continued to explain to His friends. "Be wary of every subtle trick and form of guile. An old comrade could approach in the guise of the friend he used to be. A fallen one might try to gain your sympathy as one in need of help," He said. "Perhaps there will be two of them fighting in front of you just waiting to get an advantage over you when you try to break them up. Be prepared. Be vigilant, always on the lookout. They will prowl, they will sneak around, and they will press the advance. But they will never succeed. In time, we will invade their world, and their gates will not be able to withstand our advance. They are the enemy! They no longer know life but are separated from light and life. Have no fellowship with them and the unfruitful deeds of the departed. They are death, and there is no life in them."

As the crowds began to disperse to go to their appointed

posts, the Gracious One dismissed them and informed them all that it was time for Him to confer once again.

CHAPTER NINE

The Father, the Lamb, and the Spirit of God went into solitude and remained there for quite some time. While the conference was in session, some of the angels tried to listen in and get some "intel" as to the definite purpose of the conference. The sentries at the door pressed their ears toward the door frame, attempting to pick up on any conversation sounds that might be escaping through the cracks. Some of their associates stationed down the long hallway encouraged them to listen "harder."

"Come on," Quebec said. "Push your ear up against the door."

"I can't do that. They will know what I'm doing, and I'll get caught," Cairo replied.

In the end, there was nothing to show for their efforts.

"We're all just going to have to wait for the inevitable announcement," said a resigned Quebec.

When the Mastermind emerged from Their self-imposed confinement, They possessed the blueprint for the new reality. There was something glorious and of industry for each and every being in the kingdom. There was a plan for the ages that would envelope all of creation and change the focus of every being, including the Loving One.

When the Lord God went to conference, the agenda of the meeting was the contents within the slanderous accusations leveled at Him by Lucifer. "The great God of the heavens is who He is. He knows there is no one like Him. He is the first, yet He is with the least. A loving and compassionate Judge but righteous is He," proclaimed the Spirit.

"We know these facts are known by all," the Word said. "Nevertheless, is there any doubt about this within the minds of His created beings, the loyal ones?"

The Holy Spirit added, "Lucifer was able to successfully create doubt in the minds of one-third of the angelic ranks and to persuade them to abandon God and to follow him. We must plan to let the truth of Who I Am and the falseness of his slander unfold in the lives of all to see."

"In one sense," God stated, "I felt challenged."

His character was called into question by the very recent drama and activities of his newly deposed enemy. His very being was assaulted by a far lesser person. This had to have a response. There must be an answer. Had the attack been of physical violence, where God would have had to defend Himself, that wouldn't have caused such a problem as Lucifer's slander did. "I had to allow it for all righteousness to be fulfilled," He said.

It seemed that most subjects in the kingdom could easily comprehend power and strength, especially once it had to be displayed. He could have easily subdued his assailant, and all would have understood that. But what of His love? More importantly, how could they grasp the concept of Him being love? Love was not a thing but a person. That never really made sense to the others, and God understood that.

The issues that were discussed in privacy did not only center on the verity of love; God's love, His righteousness was also in question. "If He is all powerful and can put down any rebellion or deal with any rule infraction, is that justice or tyranny?" "How can one be so just and powerful and love all at the same time?" "If He deals out justice only, that's not love, right?" "If He is all love, how can He then judge?" The two didn't really go together in the minds of the created ones. Yet the Holy One was righteous and was love all the time.

Somehow, His character had to be properly represented so that the glory due His name would be based on knowing Him for who and what He truly was. The Godhead agreed. It was a serious meeting, very solemn and extremely important. All three members were fully cognizant of the situation at hand. They had never encountered a dilemma quite like this one.

"How can the manifest attributes of love and justice be undisputed facts, known by all, to belong and rest solely in the Omnipotent One?" They asked each other.

As a result of much intense discussion, They came upon Their plan. The Father, Son, and Holy Spirit trusted each other implicitly. None of Them was ever disloyal. Yes, the Father would do anything for Their mutual good. So would the Lamb and the Spirit. This alliance was what made them One. None of Them lived for Himself but rather for the others' sake. Each was more concerned for the others' interests than for His own. Each was willing and desired to do whatever was asked in order to accomplish the great objective and fulfill their joy. There was no idea put on the discussion table that would be considered too little or too costly a price for any of Them to pay. Each would go all in, and They would express Their unity and selfless devotion one toward the others in fulfilling Their mission. God was three members yet was One.

Certain things did not have to be discussed among them. Details such as the role each had to attend to in order to accomplish the task were left to the individuals. The truth was that each member was totally devoted to His accepted task, the others' tasks, and the entire mission—even if fulfillment of it required grave personal sacrifice.

"Now that all the details have been discussed and agreed to, it is time to initiate Our idea," They agreed.

"We need to execute Our plan for the ages in Satan's domain. That is the place of our greatest challenge, and it's where we will have our greatest victory," the Father said.

"First, We must commit to reform the earth from its current matter-less void to make it inhabitable for a mortal man and all of his descendants. The man will be made to be like Us—made in Our image. He will be given dominion over all life on earth," the Spirit said.

The Word reminded them, "Satan, as he calls himself, is not going to be happy about that."

In addition to dominion, the man was also to be given the capacity to love God and also to disobey Him. The Word of God detailed cautioned. "Should he choose to disobey, then his entire life will unravel. A new power will take over his nature and turn him toward evil. At that point, he will fall in league with Satan and turn to him as the god of the world. If the man refuses to sin, he will enjoy with Us everlasting fellowship, mutual love, and endless blessings. Satan will see love on display. He will see that a mere mortal man will love God and obey Him above his capacity and desire to please himself."

"Yes," the Spirit added, "should the man choose to sin, then he will be cut off from any contact with Us. As a result, he will live in darkness and endure a death far different from the life he enjoyed with Us. No longer will he have the capacity to live on earth for all eternity. Once he is cut off from Us due to his sin, his body will begin to age and eventually wear out. When he has exhaled for his last time, his spirit will depart from his dead and decaying body, and then he will have to stand before the Judge in order to answer for what he did in his lifetime. Unless his sin is atoned for, he will be condemned as guilty and sentenced to everlasting punishment. His spirit will be cast out into a hell of torment, darkness, and eternal isolation. He will only have a memory of all the goodness of God and all his opportunities to get pardoned before his Maker that he rejected as he suffers in extreme tongue-biting pain that will go on forever," He finished.

"Our love will be evident when his sin is atoned for by the Lamb that will be slain for them," the Father continued. "All who accept and believe Our message will be pardoned. With the precious blood of an innocent victim, the stain of the guilty will be washed away. The anger of God will be assuaged, and His righteous requirements will be satisfied through the conviction, punishment, and execution of the innocent one in his place. The sinner will be washed of his guilt and set free as innocent and welcomed into everlasting joy. He will be redeemed through the sacrifice of the innocent Lamb because of the incomparable love of Jehovah."

The agreement on the plan continued. "For everyone who will come to the Lamb for forgiveness and salvation, there will be freedom, and they will be totally pardoned," said the Father. "They will satisfy the legal requirement that 'the one who sins shall die.' Without the Lamb, no one will be able to gain acquittal based on his or her own merit without suffering death. The legal standing of the sons and daughters of man as they stand before The Judge will be such that they have insufficient means to pay for their sins. Forgiveness, acquittal, and pardon will be impossible for them. They will have to pay for their evil thoughts, words, and deeds themselves, which requires death. The balance of justice will never tip in their favor, as, on the scale, they will be found wanting. Their lives as unclean and filthy offerings will not purchase the clean slate they will desire."

At that moment, the Word of God stepped forward to accomplish the will of the Lord in the lives of men and creation. He stood as one who will go in the fullness of time and live among them, as one of them, born a son but given to them as the Son of God. He would defeat sin and remain sinless. He would, at the appointed time, become the sacrifice for their atonement. He was the Lamb of God, worthy to be slain.

So the Holy Spirit moved ahead with the Word to work together with Him. The Father also joined with Them to commit to the solidarity in this grand purpose but with one last caution. "This will cost everything for You, Word. You will suffer, You will be resisted and contradicted by those You came to save. They will rail against You and finally they will arrest You, torture and condemn You to death, by hanging You on a tree. All the sin of the world will be put on You. I will turn away and forsake You as You become the sin of the world although You will know no sin. You will die and descend to Hades where You must take the keys of death from Lucifer. You will suffer horrendously there for three days and rise again to new life on the third day. You will be given a name above every name and every knee will bow to You. You will be above all god's and be seated on My right hand. All must honor You or they dishonor Me," the Father informed them.

"I will be with You, I will empower You to do all that the Father has commanded so You will prosper and be very successful in Your way," reminded the Spirit.

"I will go, I will do as You command Me and show them Your love by willingly dying in their place. All who call upon my name will be saved," volunteered the Lamb.

CHAPTER TEN

I t was time to start at the beginning. Not a single being in heaven, on earth, or under the earth had any idea what was about to happen. Neither did any know what would transpire once the plan of God was initiated. The Creator knew all that would follow and had provided everything that was necessary beforehand. The Word also knew, for He had the mind of God, being equal with the Creator. The Spirit of God was ready to go. His desire was to begin the grand plan of God, and it was the appointed time. Once this began, that would be the only business that God would be about. His truth and grand design would consume Him.

The Spirit departed and descended to the nebular below known as earth. Now the earth was formless and void. The Spirit of God hovered over the face of the deep. There was nothing there—no solid matter. It was formed of a mysterious substance, swirling particles of sticky darkness. But the Lord was going to use that ooze and those goo particles to build something good.

When the demons detected the Spirit of God's presence, they went into alarm mode. Pride boastfully yelled out, "What is He doing here? He has no business coming down here. This is our world, our domain. He has no right invading where we live."

And so the protests of the residents of the darkness continued.

But the Spirit continued to hover, waiting as if to act on cue.

Finally in the silent darkness, a Voice spoke loud and long like the mighty roar of a valiant warrior commencing his battle cry. Like the sound of an overpowering waterfall came the command:

"Let there be light."

As the Creator and the Word acted in coordination, the Spirit worked to create a brilliant even blast of bright heat energy, which transformed the earth from darkness to light in an instant.

The protesting demons, who had been preparing for war since the Spirit began to hover, were looking to attack en mass. They were all taken completely by surprise by the brightness. It had been so long since they had experienced any light. Never before had they been blasted by it as they were at this time. They began a hasty retreat into any and all of the gloomy places and shadows that could still be found. There were so many demons packed so tightly together in these isolated places that they appeared to be one monstrous contortion. They were all tangled together with swarming arms, legs, and wings in order to escape the inescapable, uncomfortable brightness and heat. God saw the light. He also saw its effect on the inhabitants. And he pronounced, "It is good."

There is only one reason He came here and did that, thought Satan, *He is looking for a conflict. If it's a fight He wants, then that is exactly what He is going to get. I will pick my time. There will be a right moment to strike. There always is. When it arrives, I will answer His invasion with a terrifying blow that will bring His scheme, whatever it is, to a deafening stillness.*

Then God, knowing what Satan was blasphemously mumbling, performed the next inexplicable feat. He separated the light from the darkness. It seems that He was giving a gift to the evil one. Satan took comfort in the darkness. He considered it "a potential asset for future use." But God pronounced it all to be good. The light on earth was called, "day," and the darkness "night."

The Lord was ready to turn his attention to the second day. So as to create and maintain order in the realm of a chaotic ruler, the Lord provided another vast separation. Having separated the day from the night on the first day, He now separated all the water and mist in the realm into two locations. He spent the whole day hammering out the separation by forming the firmament, which divided the water above from the water that was below it. The thing He used to separate the two expanses of water He also called the heavens. Above the heavens was a location for water and below them was a separate location for more water. The firmament was built above the earth like a great dome to separate the water from the water.

Prior to the division water had filled the earth in the form of vapor. *This state would make life on the planet impossible for many types of creatures that the Lord wanted to create,* God privately thought. *With the proper mixture of air and water vapor, living things on earth will have all they needed to thrive, even in this hostile kingdom.*

Knowing that He was soon to make man and all the things that would be necessary for him to live God said of all His work on that day, "It is good."

The evening came and followed the morning, and that concluded the second day.

Once again, the morning came around just like it had on the second day. Complicit and Crepe of the evil kingdom observed this together. "This event occurs at the same time each successive day. The light of the second day lasted as long as the darkness, and the succession has never changed," they both stated simultaneously.

Then God said, "Let the waters under the heavens be gathered into one place upon the earth." As the Spirit continued to hover over the forming creation, the Word applied His power to initiate and ultimately finalize the day's work.

Lucifer was not at all pleased with the way his old God had invaded his territory and was now making all these changes. "He is causing all of this commotion just as we were all getting comfortable with the darkness and chaos, and there is nothing I can do to stop it," he said in utter disgust.

Suddenly, there was a mighty stir in the firmament. As the Holy Spirit hovered over the face of creation, He poured out a blowing wind from within Himself. The sensation caught every demon in that kingdom again by shocked surprise. This event gave no advanced warning to them to prepare. They could all feel it and were terrified; it was so powerful. Many even called out in fear to God, saying, "Do not destroy us before the appointed period."

This, of course, put Lucifer into a total angry fit. "You must look to me for your salvation, not Him," he screamed at them.

He could do nothing about the wind however. There was a swirling movement of moisture and mist as it flew airborne and began gathering in large pockets of water. As the day progressed, the air felt dryer and dryer, and there appeared an increasingly large body of water in the center of the earth. It grew from puddles to being large pools to a lake and finally to a sea. Water also began forming currents on the ground as it was gathered together. Streams of water cascaded toward the ever-increasing sea, forming rivers as they gained momentum. By the middle of the lighted part of the day, virtually all the moisture and mist was removed from the atmosphere in the form of droplets and placed, ultimately, in a large ocean of water. All the water under the firmament was placed in that large body.

As this scene continued to develop, the Word spoke, "Let the dry land appear." Then the water acted as if obeying a command by the wind. It moved and shifted and rolled into deep coils. A solid place became evident as it seemed to rise up out of the recesses of the ever-deepening swirl. The land grew. Its length and width expanded until it rivaled the dimensions of the sea in terms of area.

It was quite a grand sight, and none of the fallen ones could tell what was going on or why. "We have to head for cover, or we will get washed away in that tempest," said Sloth. "He is trying to destroy us."

God knew exactly what He was doing. He was creating heaven and earth. By wisdom and knowledge He formed the foundation of the entire creation. He said that it "was good."

He was not finished yet and continued His work. God then said, "Let there be trees, grass, bushes, plants, and herbs."

As the Word commanded, so all manner of vegetation, shrubbery, and trees came into being. Each one was immediately able to bear flowers, herbs, and fruit for reproduction of its own kind. This too was good and for the good of all things yet to be created. The evening followed the day, and the third day concluded.

It's not as though anything is difficult for the great God Almighty to accomplish. The fourth day, however, was, by far, the most productive of all the days to that point. The Word said, "Let there be lights in the distant heavens to govern the day and the night." A great ball of fire appeared and began its timeless work of illuminating earth's surface from distant outer space. Like a giant power grid in the sky, the inaccessible fireball was created to provide all the light and heat for each day that the earth would need. There would be more lights added also, many more.

The great light, the sun, was then accompanied by other lesser lights. All of them were smaller in size and output as judged from the earth's vantage point. Each one produced some light as well, and each was capable of proclaiming times and seasons. Together, all of them would declare the glory of God and proclaim His plan for the ages to come.

Concerning the heavenly bodies, the Word said, "Day after day, they pour forth speech; night after night, they reveal knowledge. They have no speech. They use no words. No sound is heard from them. Yet their voice goes out into all the earth, their words to the ends of the world. In the heavens, God has pitched a tent for the sun. It is like a bridegroom coming out of his chamber, like a champion rejoicing to run his course. It rises at one end of the heavens and makes its circuit to the other. Nothing is deprived of its warmth."

The heavens declared the glory of God; the skies proclaimed the work of His hands. It was all put into place on the fourth day. If anyone carefully and collectively studied the heavens and sky they could learn from them the things that God had given them to declare—what happened, what is happening, and what will yet happen on the earth. By these, the earth would mark its calendars and observe its seasons.

There was another lesser light created to govern the earth by night. It did not generate its own light but reflected the light of the sun onto the earth. It was smaller and offered much less reliable brilliance than the greater light. It too was going to do much more than offer brightness during the night hours. It held many secrets that would be revealed only to those careful enough to observe and study it faithfully. It held a power over the earth and those who would inhabit it. Its appearance was very odd. Round and dark, it had many divots on its surface, which would be plainly visible from a great distance away. These large craters at times even gave this smaller heavenly orb the appearance of a face with eyes, a nose, a circled mouth, and even ears. The reflections of light that it rendered caused these features to look different each night.

The Creator of the universe smiled each time He looked at this moon. He delighted in showing His humor by it.

The fourth day of creation ended with the making of all the stars, planets, solar systems, and galaxies. With these in place, everything above the earth was completed. The laws governing the motion and rotation of each body had also been established.

Order was also irrevocably established, and Lucifer became wroth at the realization of order within his kingdom. He had come to a place where he only wanted chaos all the time. Time could now be marked and measured and used mightily in the lives of all created beings. Within time shall days, months, years, and entire lifetimes be contained. The first measuring tool in the life of all things would be time. The evening followed the daytime. This concluded the fourth day.

The Creator of the universe and earth was waiting and ready to get back to work the following day even before the sun shone. He was energetic and pleased to begin making the fifth day. Then He said, "Let the seas team with living creatures and the skies fill with flying animals of all kinds."

And the waters were filled with swimming, floating, jumping, diving, and schooling animals. The variety and differences among them was staggering. Large mammals, such as whales, swam in pairs, while smaller fish grouped together in tightly packed schools beyond number. Some places along the surface had a cauldron of activity—fish moving in and out of the compressed fish ball and shimmering in the bright warm sunlight. Other species were jumping high in the air and splashing back down into the water. The lively creatures played tag, chased one another through the surf and raced back and forth and up and down, as if there was no end of space in which to frolic. Everything they needed was there in the water with them. Abundant food flourished in and throughout their environment. Plants of all types were already established from their creation the day before and were readily available for all to eat.

In the heavens above, flocks of birds darted and fluttered, dive-bombed, and flew. Just for the exhilaration and the thrill of it, they stayed in the air for hours. They went this way and then that way—east, west, south, and north, everywhere in the vast expanse.

In the midday, creatures below could experience a shade of darkness in the bright day. Suddenly, the sun would disappear behind a massive swarm of birds passing by. So thickly packed together was the collection of them that sunlight was blocked and partially obscured from those below. The light could hardly get through the numbers and had to squeeze its way through the mass to reach the ground. Then gradually, the lightness would increase with the passing of the large flock. On some occasions, this drama would repeat throughout the day, for the populations, variety, and activity of the sheer numbers of birds was overwhelming.

Then God said to all the living things in the water and the air, "Be fruitful and multiply. Fill the whole earth and the seas with your offspring. Each type of animal must reproduce with its own kind. Male and female have I made you. This is the natural order of creation."

Everything understood exactly what He wanted, for obedience was built into these creations. Fruitfulness was then going to happen. Being fruitful always pleased the Maker. Thus ended the evening and morning, the fifth day.

CHAPTER ELEVEN

At the dawn of the sixth day, God started making more living creatures. He made cattle, cats of all kinds, large and small reptiles, insects, bears, swift and light deer, moose, small creeping animals, and large animals—some very large. Each one was set to roam the earth and make living places in every field, tree, bush, ravine, hill, hole, cave, marsh, and meadow. They too were given the command, "Be fruitful and multiply." This directive came as a blessing. And in following it, all the animals would enjoy the best that God had offered.

The Lord God looked at all that He had made. He thoroughly enjoyed watching it all and interacting with His creatures. All of the animals enjoyed Him just the same and would, at times, show off for Him during their fun and games. Fish would leap out of the water as high as they could go. Birds would perform aerial acrobatics. Even the four-footed animals would run, jump high, or climb impossible angles just for Him. He watched it all with pure enjoyment.

But as He compared all that He had accomplished with the blueprint and grand plan that He had made, He knew that there was still very important work to be done. The final piece, the grandest moment of His work was still yet to be made. He still had to make something special—*someone* special. By this final piece, He would demonstrate His love for all, and He would be known. There would never again be anyone who could falsely accuse Him whose accusations He could not disprove with a point of His finger.

With plenty of time still left in the day, God spoke the most profound sentence that creation has ever heard: "Let Us make man in Our own image." At once, a more serious tone came through his voice and the look in His eye.

He immediately followed that pronouncement by turning His gaze upon the ground. They were one in this task as Father, Son, and Holy Spirit are one in everything They thought, did, and said. Just as each person in the Godhead was totally devoted and committed to the success and joy of the others, so in unity God made man.

Out of the clay dirt, God piled a mound of earth and began carving it into the shape of the first man, who He was to name Adam. He elongated the pile so that it was about six feet from top to bottom. Then He began molding the head and neck of the man, followed by the shoulders, arms, and hands with fingers. Next came the man's midsection and the completed shape of his body and legs. The upper half had a tapered effect from shoulder to waist. The lower half of the man had joined the upper half at the waist. Here, the two legs began and lengthened downward, ending at two feet with five toes each, one for each leg.

The man was lying down during his creation, but once completed, he was designed to stand upright on his feet and walk. During his formation, the Word spoke into the man in order to create the intricate, delicate inner organs. These things were hidden from view but crucial for the life of the person. All of the functions of these organ systems demonstrated a design so brilliant, so intelligent that future offspring would take months to form.

Carefully, He worked. Long into the day and then into the afternoon he continued, making sure everything was just right—perfect.

One thing that the Holy One had planned for the man that

would be very special was an ability to use his mind. The man was also given the most intricate organ of all in its design, function, and performance. With his brain, the first man would be able to name, sort, plan, organize, categorize, orchestrate, design, create, feel, express, and communicate. Within the mind and brain's capacity would be capabilities and worlds that the animals could never actualize. The Spirit noted, "Their coordinated function is essentially the one thing that will separate him from them. With the use of his mind and mental reasoning powers, he will be able to match them in everything and much, much more."

The form and features of the man were completed, and his body continued to lie prostrate in the soil at the Lord's feet. *When he is made to stand up, everything that is and will be is going to change dramatically*, the Lord thought. It was not just creation that would be impacted by his presence and life force; so too would God, eternity, and Satan. When the man was made to stand up, he would be a threat to all of the agents of this once-dark world. While he was in communion with the great God, he would be an ambassador where he lived for the other kingdom that he had never seen or been to. More than anything, he would represent the King, Whom he would see. Not only would he delight in the King's love, he would also rejoice to know Him and to do His will.

The thought of all this gave the Mighty Creator a serene contentment that effervesced into a glow. A smile ran all across His face. He could easily envision all that the man could and would do. In this person, God would finally have someone to love to the utmost. But also, possibly, the man would demonstrate a love for his Creator too. This was the moment that He had waited so long for.

After a deep inhale, the One Who was ever true then breathed into the nose and mouth of the man. Instantly, a warmth coursed through his entire body. Blood began to flow, the heart pumping rhythmically as it pushed the oxygen-enriched life fluid through his veins. A new, vibrant living color came into his once grayish tone. His fingers and then his toes began to wiggle. His eyes began to flutter and then opened, and as they focused for the first time, the man saw the brilliant, beaming face of the Loving God smiling at him.

For a moment, and then a moment longer, the Father was speechless. The Word was unable to utter more than a sound at the inner feelings that overwhelmed Him. His heart also raced and thumped wildly in His soul as a flooding tide of emotion washed over Him again and again. He tried to speak, but the words came out haltingly, unintelligibly. He took a moment to compose Himself, and then, He simply said, "Hello," in a soft, gentle tone barely above a whisper.

For the man, it was much easier to give his reply to this initial greeting. "Hello," he answered.

Upon hearing this, God broke out into a loud, long, unrestrained laugh that went on uncontrolled for much longer than any laughter He had ever had before. It was a laugh of joy but also of longing fulfilled and, most of all, victory. All of creation immediately stopped for a period to take direct and personal notice and to determine what it was that had made their Love so indefatigably happy.

Finally, He gained control of His expressive mirth and told the man, "Go ahead and stand up."

God saw that the man was not sure how to get to his feet. Gently the loving, laughing one held out His hand and grabbed the man's hand and helped him up.

A strange transformation occurred within the once still, lifeless man. As he received God's breath and then heard His Word and felt His being, he too became a living soul. He was now far more different than the animals and even the angels than ever before—for he had a capacity to choose to obey his Maker. He could choose to love light, life, and good for their own sakes and not simply for what benefit he got from them. He could choose. Being made with a spirit, mind, and body, he became like the triune God and would forever fellowship with and represent Him there on the earth.

"You will have work to do, assigned tasks to complete, and duties to manage. I am giving dominion over the earth and its creatures to you." This statement, made by God, cast a supreme importance into the life and work of the man. "You will decide what is permitted and what is not permitted upon the earth," God clarified for him.

CHAPTER TWELVE

Satan's agents, Sloth and Glutton, were nearby as all of this introduction unfolded. Silently, they watched and quietly commented. "He was never that happy before, certainly not when He ever interacted with us. He never treated us so happily as He is treating this creature He is talking to," Sloth said.

"Yeah, what is it anyway?" Glutton replied.

Envy flew in to join the conversation. "What is the big deal about that weak-looking thing?" he chimed in.

The next thing they heard sent chills of fear down their demonic bodies. God gave the man the dominion mandate. They discussed among themselves what that meant. What did he mean when He said, "You will have dominion over everything"? It sure sounded like there was going to be a lot of trouble with this walking creature that the Almighty was talking to.

The three demons decided that they had better take this latest development back to Lord Satan. Perhaps he would be able to make heads or tails out of all that had just transpired.

All of the scouts flew out of there and into Satan's presence. They were panicked, and panting wildly and totally out of breath with fear when they arrived.

Impatiently Satan waited. "Come on, come on. What is it?" he demanded.

Finally, they were able to get intelligible sentences out in order to give him the news. "Lord Satan," Envy began, "the king in heaven came here again today. And this time, He made a creature that looks a lot like Him. The creature can talk, think, feel, and understand. The king then gave that thing He called 'man' dominion over this entire kingdom of ours."

Upon hearing this, Satan was initially stunned. He was apoplectic and just stared in stone silence as he processed the news. He was initially unable to function.

The messengers stared at each other, waiting and hoping their leader could recover in order to figure out their next move.

Sometime later, Satan regained his senses and was very irate. "Dominion? He gave him dominion? He can't do that! This is my world, my kingdom, my domain. I'm in charge here, and I won't stand for this creative meddling from the enemy and His new little sidekick. He's obviously not abiding by my rules or our understanding. And He is pushing for a war."

Gradually, Satan began to settle down and collect his thoughts. He sent Envy with a message. He was told to call for a meeting of all the higher-level demons, who were to report at once.

Glutton and Sloth wanted to go too, but Satan forbade them, saying they were too slow.

"There has been an invasion into our world, and we must do something about it," was Envy's cry.

"What?" was a common reply.

As this summons went out, everyone in the realm of Lord Satan knew not to miss it. In fact, every demon showed up, whether invited or not. Most meetings were extremely boring, mundane, and of no consequence. But this one had the makings of an exciting event, and none of the "underlings" could get there fast enough.

It didn't take long for the masses to figure out that the announced meeting was the place to be. All the demons who were somebody were going, and none of them wasted any time in getting there. In fact, all of the citizens of the dark kingdom were arriving early. So the proceedings began ahead of schedule, and most in the crowd could sense a rare opportunity within this unexpected disaster.

"There is such a collective energy in the room," Merchury said. "It is certain to result in many great ideas."

Pride and Greed agreed and already had thoughts that they wanted to make public so they could get credit and move up the ladder of power. "Maybe we can move up the demonic power structural chain if we can just score big with our great scheme," said Greed.

"Yeah, if Lust or Envy don't steal our idea and get the credit that we should get," Pride answered.

The fact was that most of the demons were still trying to get Satan to realize their value to him. When they had hatched their plan in heaven, they had all thought that their usefulness to him was an ironclad reality. *Imagine Lucifer wanting me, needing me, and choosing me*, had been their universal thought. "It made joining his cause so much easier," muttered Giteven. Now they knew that it was another lie, and those days were long gone. Each one was expendable and felt as if they were nothing but a tool in his hand—"unless I can score big and actually reach that level in Satan's eyes," many of the lesser demons argued.

Passionately, Satan spoke to them all about the sixth day's events, revealing the facts had been reported to him by Sloth, Glutton, and Envy. The crowd booed in disapproval of that day and every day before it. Intently each one listened and instinctively knew that this was a time for thought.

Satan challenged them all by saying, "Think it out. What is going on? What is the Devious One up to? Why did He even bother making such a weak creature with far fewer powers than any of us? Since He was not happy with us, what makes Him think that He will be happy with that one?"

The questions and spitball answers continued until one of them began to grasp the meaning of all that was happening. Giteven, a usually quiet demon, was finally given a chance to speak. "Remember, Lord Satan, as Lucifer, you challenged God and rose up against Him. You told Him that He was not loving and was nothing but a cruel dictator," he said. Of course they all remembered that moment, which seemed so long ago. "It seems like forever ago. Maybe it was,' Giteven said, reminiscing. "In large part, perhaps that action you took then and the resulting attitude that it prompted in Him is why we are here and having this meeting. It seems rather likely that Lucifer's diatribe was the motivation for this attack on our kingdom. It must be that He is speaking to you, Satan. You have been replaced as the joy of His life, the apple of His eye. He is going to love that creature and give everything to him to show you how wrong you are."

Then Satan said, "You might be right, little fella. I will tell you what I'm going to do. I will spy on that thing until I understand everything about it. I will know him, how his Creator relates to him, what they talk about, and where he is vulnerable. I will find out where to strike, when and how, and in so doing, I will destroy God's whole great scheme. The only one that will be talking then will be me, and I will be saying, 'How do you like me now?'" As he said that, Satan gyrated his hips and broke out into in unchoreographed series of dance moves that brought the whole hall into raucous guffaws and roaring laughter.

The more they laughed, the longer he danced and kept on chanting, "How do you like me now? How do you like me now?"

The crowd exploded into frenzied approval.

Finally, Satan ran out of breath and stopped the exhibition. When he was finished recovering from his panting fit, he adjourned the meeting.

As was their custom following a large meeting, all who were

present could be heard speaking to their fellow comrades as they exited that strange meeting place. "Boy that Creator just made another huge mistake, another screw up. First He had to pick a fight with all of us and then kick us out. Then He created this place with all the recent changes, and now He put that thing here. To top it all off, He gave that new thing charge over all of it, even us. How stupid can He be?" Pride said to Giteven. "We are not going to listen to that creature He just made. And with our latest plan forming, the Creator is certainly doomed to fail."

Giteven replied animatedly, "Oh, this is going to be exciting." And he rubbed his claws together as he spoke.

CHAPTER THIRTEEN

Immediately following his departure from the hall, Satan flew to the place where God and the creature were last seen together. In order not to be noticed, he disguised himself as a slithery reptile. In that disguise, he could crawl around, low to the ground, and conceal himself as he got close enough to see and hear them. The vegetation was so lush and the leaves so full, it was easy to remain out of view to both of them. Besides that, he just looked like a common animal. So what harm can he be?

Wow, those two have been together for a long time, he thought. He had anticipated that the interaction between the Creator and His new creation would be over before too long, as had usually been the case when he used to meet with the Maker. He was there watching much longer than he had ever thought would be necessary. The two worked, played, ran, and joked. At the end of the evening, they sat and talked some more.

Wow, He is still not leaving. He is just being there with it. What is going on here? Satan was feeling offended again.

He overheard God telling the creature that he needed his own name. This was where it all got very interesting. The Lord spoke to his companion and told him, "This place we are in is your garden. You are so very precious and special to Me, and I will always be with you. I have longed for this day even before there were any days."

Then God gave the man a job. "Name all of the animals. Whatever you name it, that is what it will be called."

The companion still needed a name. Up to that point, the

Lord had just called him "friend." The conversation continued until the Lord reminded His friend, "I formed you out of the dust of the earth. Therefore, you are man. Your name will be Adam."

After naming His friend, God told Adam, "There is something of utmost importance that I must tell you."

Adam turned to look at his Maker.

"Look at Me, Adam," God said, wanting him to make eye contact. "It is critical that you understand what I am going to say next."

Adam gazed into His eyes. This time he saw a somber and a most sincere expression on His face. "Yes, Lord, I am listening," Adam replied.

God waited and then began His message. "It is My pleasure to give everything to you. I give you My entire kingdom. It is yours, and we will be together. Nothing gives Me greater happiness than being with you."

There was a pause as Adam waited for Him to continue.

"There is one tree, however, that you must not eat from—that one there in the middle of the garden."

Adam looked at the specific tree God was pointing to and said, "Okay."

God explained, "If you eat from that tree, you will cease to live. You will die." The Lord now looked as if He was on the verge of weeping. "But you can eat from every other tree in the garden. Enjoy them all. They are for you. But not that one," He said and pointed to the forbidden tree again.

Adam felt uncomfortable looking at God this way, but He insisted that he do it. Adam replied, "I won't eat from that tree, just as You commanded."

Satan couldn't believe what he was witnessing. *It's as if the friend is perfectly suited to make Him happy, and He is all that the friend needs and nothing more.*

And it was so. With the passing of the morning and now the evening, this ended the sixth day.

CHAPTER FOURTEEN

The sun splashed its warming light on the earth for the seventh time. This day, all attention was not going to be on the earth and all the changes that were going to be done to it but on God. And it was not at all about what He was going to do. Instead, the focus and interest of the observers, in heaven and on earth, concerned what He was not going to be doing.

There was no further need for more creation. He crowned His own efforts with the ultimate achievement. By His wisdom, knowledge, and understanding, the Lord founded and built a beautiful universe with the focal point being His new friend. Everything was so good. God made all that was seen and unseen. He made every necessary law and the natural processes by which He would govern His creation.

Adam would care for it, but not on this day. The seventh day was to be a day of rest.

So that was what they did. Adam didn't feel a need to rest all day but did it out of obedience to his God.

The morning and the evening concluded the seventh day. When God looked upon the completed creation He said, "It is good." And it was finished.

The first day of the second week arrived, with Adam preparing his morning meal. He had already discovered the delicious taste of many fruits and nuts and decided which ones would suffice for this meal. Satan was also up and watching. Like a stealthy cat, he observed his presumed victim carefully and unceasingly.

Without prying, he watched. Yet with skillful scrutiny, he never took his eyes off of him. He remained motionless and still, like a hidden rock, very present yet undetected. Satan had a job to do and was undeterred in using all the skills he had ever possessed to succeed.

The man was going to be busy that day too. He had a job to do that required all of his powers of observation, inquiry, language, vocabulary, management, memory, and description.

The first thing Adam did in the morning was set up a platform from which to work, and then he waited. He was there alone with no one to help him, so he wasn't entirely sure if he was doing it right. Suddenly, animals started walking right up to him while he was sitting there on his platform. Just a few came at first. Then gradually, increasingly, more and more came at a time.

The Lord of beasts was sending them to him to be given a name. Every type of animal created and given the command to be fruitful and multiply after its own kind was told to go to Adam. The birds flew in, four-footed animals walked there, some slithered, and others crawled. They came right to him.

Satan watched as Adam named each kind. *And in so doing, he is exercising his dominion*, Satan thought.

Satan then considered walking up to him alone as the reptile to get a closer look but noticed the deftness with which Adam could evaluate the animal's traits and thought better of it. *He might understand what I am and discuss it with his Friend, and I could lose my advantage*, he decided.

Adam investigated each pair of animals, one by one. He rubbed his hands over their heads, backs, legs, and tails if they had one. He made mental notes of each kind's characteristics. He smelled each one, taking in its uniqueness of odor. He enjoyed listening the sound that each animal made and appreciated the way most of them could make many different noises. Some growled. Others chirped. There were different kinds of roars, bellows, trumpet sounds, high-pitched squeals, grunts, moans, clicks, barks, purrs, and giggles.

The first day on the job for Adam was intense and yet very fulfilling to him. It was very noticeable that each male had a female companion. And each was unique, yet they bore many similarities to each other.

As Adam progressed through his day's work of naming the animals, an unknown feeling slowly encroached upon him. As he saw the pairs together, each with its own mate, how they related to each other, did things together, and shared what they had in common, he wondered. *Each animal seems to live not only with its companion but also for it. What about me?*

The thought would not dissipate. *How could I think such a thing? God is my companion, my friend. He is never distant*, he rebuked himself.

Then, why this feeling? He experienced an emotion, a longing for something that seemed to be missing—for someone. It felt as though a piece of him was never added, that he was not complete. *I will have to ask my Father about all of this soon.*

Adam was fast becoming very intimate with his Maker. For him, it was never an issue to be trusting or being totally open in the conversation. Adam knew that God knew him completely. He understood that God had made him out of the dust and breathed the breath of life into him. He also knew why God made him. "For continuous fellowship and love," he mumbled.

This knowledge had a substance to it. It was almost tangible— like the warmth from the glow of a fire. But there was a limit to the depth of his knowing and what Adam had learned of his Maker. Enjoying each new level of intimacy with his Father and striving to know more was the true objective in the love affair.

Adam told himself that he felt satisfied that God knew him

thoroughly and that he was getting ever closer to Him. In this transparency, there was nothing he could not discuss—no subject he felt could not be brought up.

As he thought, he eventually considered that, since his Friend already knew him, *Maybe it was Him Who prompted this new realization in my heart.* Was Adam the only one of his kind? *Will God be making any other living souls? Why does each animal have a mate and was told to be fruitful and multiply but I don't and can't?*

Adam decided that the subject had to be brought up soon and that the next day would be the time when he would do it. He only hoped that the same skill and tactfulness he'd used in naming the animals could be utilized properly in handling this upcoming interview. *I sure don't want to upset Him.*

There were still so many things to learn about from his Father. *I know that I have never even scratched the surface of the knowledge of the Almighty. Perhaps it's a personal characteristic of mine to want to know Him more than I do.*

Adam had a very active and inquisitive mind. He said, "I should learn my own character traits at least as well as I learned the animals' when I named each one."

It still had not dawned on him that God always watched him. In those times during the day when Adam thought that he was alone, God was actually there with him.

Unbeknownst to Adam, the Lord had noted, "It is not good for man to be alone." The all loving one said, "I see the dull feeling of loneliness in Adam. I am going to give him a beautiful gift. It is going to have to cost him something of value."

Adam was going to have to give something of his to make it happen. In time, Adam would agree that the trade-off was well worth his sacrifice. It was time for Adam to get his helpmate, and he would be so happy once he received this beautiful gift that he would never miss what he exchanged for her in the process.

As the day came to a close, the Creator clapped His hands, rubbed them together, and said, "Tomorrow is going to be a big day."

Once again, the sun shone early in the morning hours and stirred the man to awaken to his daily responsibilities. With nervous determination, he rose up from his bed and prepared for his all-important meeting with God. He anticipated, *I will most likely be the one who determines the course of our upcoming interactions. Of course*, he thought, *I have no idea which way it will go once I arrive for our daily visit and the subject actually gets brought up.*

The Lord always arrived in the morning hours when it was still cool out, and He never left in a hurry. The visits were always enriching to both parties, even though Adam noticed that they were never planned out or scripted. Rather, as they conversed, their interactions were spontaneous and relevant. They never ended before an hour had passed and often continued well into the afternoon.

This one is going to be a little different, Adam thought. He was bringing the agenda, with hopes of convincing God of what he thought would be best for him. *There is no reason to fear*, he told himself. *He is so good.* And although he wasn't sure how the discussion would go, he knew no harm would befall him. *I just don't want Him to be offended.* This was his main reservation. Whether his request would be approved or not, he was uncertain. But he was sure that he too needed a companion like himself; it was his heart's desire. He was very nervous but hoped that he could give a convincing argument toward that end.

Without any fanfare, the Lord Omnipotent arrived in the garden while it was still early and cool. When Adam came into His presence, there was the usual joy of being together but also a slightly tense apprehension within Adam.

Of course the One Who sees all could sense it and, with concern, said, "Tell Me, Adam. What is it that's bothering you?" He questioned the nature of Adam's reluctance.

After a deep breath and a hard swallow, the man began his request by setting up the context. "I named the animals and had some unexpected experiences while doing that," he said, adding, "At times I tried to relate to them in a similar way that they did with each other while they were there at the platform. Then I realized that it could not be done. There is no connection between me and any of them. The animals also seemed to know," he said. "The work of naming them left me with a growing realization that each pair of animals belongs together without me and that I had no one. This left a hollow and empty feeling in my soul."

He continued to unravel his feelings before his Father. And as he did, what he said was nothing like he had rehearsed.

Then the Lord summarized Adam's comments, "So you're saying that you feel incomplete."

"Yes, sort of. But, of course, I cherish the time we spend together. I just have a need that I think is leaving me with an emptiness when I'm not with You." Adam paused to pick a low-hanging fruit. He was hungry from not eating anything before he'd left for their time together. He offered one to the Lord, Who happily accepted it. He continued, "I don't want to convey the idea that I don't cherish each morning or that they're not important to me because of the time we spend together."

Adam admitted that he did not know exactly what he was longing for or what it should look like, feel like, or act like. He also did not know how God could help him or even if He would. They had discussed so many things within their friendship and were quite intimate, so Adam was still fearful that what he was saying would be hurtful to his Friend. *Somehow, I need to indicate that this is not a rejection but an addition to our relationship that would bring value*, he thought.

Adam went on in his attempt to verbally escort his Friend away from any wrong conclusion so that, when he was finished, he could look at his Friend and see the face of understanding and, hopefully, a desire within Him to provide for this need.

To his amazement, after he had completely finished his presentation, he looked and saw a smile on the face of God. "I can do something about this. But it will cost you something of value to you. It will be worth it of course," God said, comforting him.

To Adam's pleasant surprise, this request actually pleased the Lord very much. And the two went on to discuss this next project during the remainder of the day.

God explained exactly what he planned to do in order to bring the project to completion. "Your request won't be met by using clay like I used in creating you. Instead, the answer comes from Me using a part of you, Adam. There is going to be a procedure where the foundation that will be used to fashion your companion will come from your own body. We are going to work together, and I am going to extract it from you." The Lord spared no detail in his explanation.

Adam listened intently and did not shrink back from what he had to do so that this could be accomplished. "I am all in and ready to get it done," he assured God.

The Father then said, "It is decided then that this event will occur the next day and that We will begin early in the morning."

Adam was getting ready to leave the encounter, having no idea what tomorrow would be like during the procedure. Then God spoke. "He really has no idea what the future, after the procedure, will be like with a helpmate." God of course did know. He told Adam, "I am very happy for you."

He could see by His Spirit that there would be consequences that produced damage this world would not heal from. God knew that. He also knew of the joy and the glory that would come to Him and to Adam as well.

As God looked forward in time, past the next morning's scheduled event, He could see what was sure to follow. "The results of this decision will truly cost Us," He said.

"It will cost The Father the very best and most precious thing that He has," agreed the Spirit.

The next morning, both the man and his Lord were up and present together before the sun lit up the morning sky. The previous day, they had decided upon the place where the procedure would take place. God again explained exactly how He was going to create His friend's new wife as He called her.

Adam wondered, *Just how bad is it going to hurt?*

Then the Doctor told him that he would place him in a deep sleep, as if sending him on a distant voyage. Then God would work on just his body. Throughout the entire operation, Adam would not feel a thing.

But the pain, oh the pain that would follow.

They walked together to the designated area, and God told Adam, "Lie down."

Once in the prone position, the Lord plucked some leaves from a nearby plant and squeezed them until drops of liquid were produced. He then had his patient open his mouth and dropped a few droplets down into the back of Adam's throat.

Shortly after that, the man was sound asleep, unresponsive to any and all stimuli. To this day, it is not known exactly how it was done, but the Lord surgically removed a rib from Adam and, with it, created his female companion. "Now We have made man in Our image. Male and female, made We them."

Following the surgery, Adam was stiff and sore and took a few days of rest from his daily responsibilities in order to recover. He and his companion spent that time getting to know each other intimately.

Adam's heart was absolutely full. He was in love with his Creator, he had the most lovely and beautiful companion who was the envy of all in the animal kingdom, and he got to be with each of his two loves each day.

A few days after his surgery, he returned to his exhilarating work in the garden. He was going to live for eternity in this place, and he always said, "These current conditions will never grow old. Living in this paradise will never be mundane or boring." Adam was always going to love the life he had been given, especially now that he had his "completer" at his side.

It didn't take long for Adam to realize that he'd named every animal on the earth that had come to him within the garden. He also had a name of his own, given to him by his Father. His new mate had no name, however, and that could not stand any longer. He directed his thoughts to this next matter and considered all the variables that needed to be taken into account. *She was created from one of my own body parts, so she came from me. Since I am man, then she shall be called woman*, his mind concluded.

Having thought his work was finished, he took his mate, his companion to his house, and in their relations she became his wife. Unlike the man, however, she still had no real name.

CHAPTER FIFTEEN

I t was now common and expected that the light from the sun would shine early to mark the beginning of the new day. On the first day after Adam and his companion had become husband and wife, Adam planned on taking her around and through the garden. It was very important to orient her so she would become familiar with the place where their lives would be lived together forever. His objective was for her to have the same thoughts and feelings about each tree, rock, nest, burrow, animal, smell, and sound as him. "I have to show you everything that I have had any interaction with, so we can share it together," he told her. As he led her by the hand through his domain, he passionately described his experience and history with each location and living thing.

She was just as eager to become fully acquainted with each and every facet of the garden. "Let's take time every day for that," she said, "so we can keep learning all there is to know about our home."

He sincerely wanted the events and scenery as he showed them to her to elicit in her the same devotion he had. He shared everything with her, in hopes that the two of them could mutually enjoy each and every thing together for an ever-endearing oneness.

And he saved the best for last. She still had to see the beautiful spot where he rose from the ground after the breath of life was given to him. He was going to take her to his other most favorite places. One place that was very important to show her in particular was the place where he'd set up the platform that he sat upon when the animals came to him. Yes he had given each type of animal their name that very day, but he also got to know them individually.

"It was there where I realized and felt the sense of needing a helpmate too," he explained to his new love. "The animals came to me in pairs, so I had firsthand knowledge that each animal had a mate. The male had the female, and the female had a male companion. Each pair seemed to complete each other. But for me there was no fulfillment equal to what I saw in the animals. My heart began to fill with a strange emptiness. I looked over in the direction where I frequently met God, and I wondered," he told her.

"There was also a cool place where I would go every morning, and my Friend would be there waiting for me." Adam described as vividly as he was able the encounters, the interactions, and the feelings he shared with God during those daily visits. There was yet another place or two that she had to see among the many he planned to show her. There was, for example, the place where that tree was.

As they walked hand in hand through the garden, he would pick certain fruits that were his favorites from the best trees. He would take a bite and then hand the fruit to her. She would notice the look of delight on his face, so she would also take a bite and be thrilled with all the delightful flavors. Then she would gush with the overflowing pleasure that being with "her man" gave her.

As they continued to walk, they talked about everything that they did and saw. At times, a friendly animal would cross their path, looking to say hello in its own manner. "Oh, isn't he just so adorable," she would say. Together, they would giggle at the animal, not knowing that their bliss was more about being complete with each other than the animal itself.

Finally, they reached the most important destination. From

that vantage point, he could show her two separate trees. "One of those trees," he told her, "is the tree of life. The other is the forbidden tree." In front of that tree, he recounted to her the conversation he'd had with their Maker about the fruit of that tree. It was called the tree of the knowledge of good and evil, he told her and, "It is the only tree that we can't eat from," he said. "God told me this, and now I'm telling you not to eat the fruit from that tree."

He was very stern, and she took a mental note of how his look of delight turned to stark seriousness.

She questioned, "Why is that? It seems just like the other trees."

Adam looked at her intently and told her to look at him. In all seriousness, he said, "The Lord told me that, if I or you ever eat from it, we will die the death."

"Oh my," she said. "That is dreadful."

So he said, "Tell me that you'll never take the fruit or even touch this tree—that you will stay away from it. Can you tell me that?"

At that moment, she solemnly vowed to him that she wouldn't ever eat its fruit or even touch the fruit from the tree. Before they left that place and moved on to the other interesting locations on his itinerary they gave each other a big reassuring hug.

CHAPTER SIXTEEN

Unbeknownst to Adam and his wife, Satan was spying on them, blended into the scenery to look like a branch on a nearby tree. He heard every word they said and noted the urgency of their tones. "Hmm," he mumbled to himself. "I think my opportunity to strike has presented itself here." He quickly fled the scene to put all of his subjects on notice that there was going to be an emergency meeting that evening.

It was a raucous crowd that assembled later that night. Satan organized the event in the largest room with the best acoustics in the entire netherworld. This was not only going to be an information-giving meeting, it was also a celebration of their upcoming victory.

"For far too long have we sat helplessly by as that puny little creature exercised his dominion," Satan spat into the crowd, "within our demonic territory. How we have waited for him to slip up so that we could catch him in a vulnerable position and slit his throat."

"Oh, how we have all wanted to kill him," yelled Assassin.

Now that he had his helpmate, Satan was even more nauseous with fury and distain. "Once again that phony trickster created something in my world without even asking for my permission," the devil bellowed. "I will pay Him back for his treachery and violation of our 'understanding.' He will pay!" Satan threw his podium through the air and smashed it against the far wall.

The crowd was starting to get edgy and began yelling in approval of Satan's continued boasts.

"That little imp of His was given my authority, and now it turns out that he has a little love object."

The crowd chanted, "Kill her. Kill her. Kill her now!"

"Won't that be just peachy when I get her to walk to her own death and willingly join us as an enemy of God and her darling husband?" Satan said, revealing his plan.

"Tell us, tell us. What did you discover?" many of the demons shouted. "How can we finally find a way to destroy them?"

"I was spying on them as I always do and heard them discuss the fruit from the tree in the middle of the garden. No one told us that fruit will bring about their deaths if only they eat it. But now isn't that nice to know. He thought they could keep it a secret. It turns out our little lovesick Creator wants to test them with that tree to find out if they will always love Him."

The massive crowd began chanting another phrase. "Hate Jehovah. Hate Jehovah. Hate Jehovah."

"The man and woman had a long disgusting conversation about how they will never touch that tree, and she vowed to him that she will never eat its fruit. But eat it she will!"

The room exploded with a victory cry in the hailing of Lord Satan.

"After we have turned her against them, even His little buddy will turn on Him and impale Him when he chooses to eat the fruit too. I will knock out two problems with one fruit, and it only takes one small deception to bring that whole scheme to an agonizing end. The ever joyful King will weep and gnash His teeth with the misery of His failure."

"Death to His plan," they all chanted.

"And on to our final victory," replied Satan.

And the millions broke out into their victory chant in earnest.

The Lord discussed the events of the distant past with Adam and his wife. "Even when Lucifer lived in glory with God, along with all of the angels, he was full of guile and deception. He was a liar and the father of all lies. After he was convicted of treasonous perfidy, he was ejected out of heaven to the lower regions of the galaxy and into the formless void of earth. All of his own godlike attributes then morphed into villainy by gargantuan proportions. He is the most deceptive being in the entire creation. Be careful," He warned, "for he might plan on using that talent in his efforts against the woman."

Satan was going to enact a simple yet effective strategy against her that would get her to bring the death that God had promised. "By the use of the lie, I am personally going to see to it that she does eat the fruit from the forbidden tree. She does not even personally know of me, and that detail is sure to come in handy. The easiest time to work against people is when they don't even know you are there," he told Decapo.

"Now she is the center of your entire campaign efforts to regain your place on earth from them by force. After the plan gets completely unfurled, she will think of you every day until she dies," Decapo added. He continued with a word of caution. "In spite of this grand design and the apparent likelihood that you will vanquish her, she does have one undeniable defense—the Word of God. She knows what He said. If she just remembers it and applies it to any encounter you have with her, then she will surely prevail."

Satan knew that too, but he replied that he was counting on his ability to twist what God said. "I will get her to doubt and, finally, to agree with me before she inflicts her own fatal wound," he told him.

So he waited and waited. Every day, he set himself in a good position near the tree in question and patiently waited for her. *Someday she will wander over here*, he thought, *by herself, without the man nearby to meddle into our conversation.*

Many days passed without any encounter between the two. Finally, it happened. As she approached his direction, his heart began thumping. *Who could have known that such a devastating trail of fateful events could transpire on such a beautiful peaceful day*, he thought. *But then again, such a backdrop of scenery is perfect for this victim to be off guard and prone to fall.*

As his many underlings often said to each other, "Lord Satan is many things, but above all, he is an enemy of God. His hatred for the one who created him is demonstrably the primary motivation for him being able to patiently wait for a strike. He is so certain that he is going to succeed that nothing toward that end seems to be any more than an inconvenience to him."

One way Satan would describe himself is a master of disguise. "I am certain I could stand before anybody or get into and out of any situation without it even being known that I was ever there," he would brag. "I can be almost anything or anybody at any time. This ability gives me more pleasure and satisfaction than all the others that I possess. By it, I am able to convince anybody into thinking that I am what I really am not. It's an ability that is not essential to getting what I want. I mean, I do have other tactics to use that are also very effective. Perhaps, that is why I get such pleasure from using deceptive disguises. With very little effort, I can prevail." That was the method he decided would work best against his anticipated victim.

The choice for him was obvious. "Since the reptile disguise recently worked so well, this time I will consume and control the body of one of the nearby serpents. They are very subtle and cunning. Many times have I seen them almost matching wits with Adam in his daily pursuits as garden keeper. It's an easy choice to make, the only logical one that I could come to," he had explained to Glutton, Greed, Lust, and Envy.

So Satan possessed the body of one of the most colorful

serpents he could find. When the woman finally came near him, her presence was a call to action, and he set his plan in motion.

Standing by a leafy green juniper tree, the serpent held one of his pickings from the tree of the knowledge of good and evil and waited for the unsuspecting woman to get close enough for a conversation. When she reached the strike point, he held out the fruit and asked her, "Would you like to have a bite to refresh yourself from your day of hard labor?"

"Well, that looks like the fruit that grows on the forbidden tree," she said. "Don't you know that you are not allowed to eat that?"

"Oh, it is from that tree for sure, and it is delicious," he said. "I have eaten from every tree in this garden and can attest to the fact that no fruit from any other tree can rival that tree's fruit for color; freshness; aroma; texture; and, most of all, taste."

"Don't you know what that fruit will do to you?" the woman replied. "It will cause you to die the death."

Satan answered, "Do I look dead to you? Do you even know what death is? You can plainly see that I've been eating this. It's almost gone. In fact, I have eaten from that tree many times. Who told you not to eat its fruit? Probably someone who wants it all for Himself."

She replied that her husband, Adam, had told her that God had strictly warned him not to eat anything from that tree. "All the fruit from any other tree is permissible," she said. "But eating that fruit will cause us to die."

Seeing his opportunity, the serpent continued his line of questioning. "Did God tell you not to eat from that tree?" he asked in his derisive tone.

"In fact," she said, "He said not to eat from it or even touch it." The woman tried to convince him of her certainty of what God had said and her total belief in its truth.

But that cunning serpent noted yet another inaccuracy in what she had said, so he pressed yet further.

"This fruit obviously won't kill you. Instead, it will make you wise like God. You will understand both good and evil," he said. "If you eat it, you will become like God." He held out the fruit again for her to take, and he asked, "Want some?"

She stared at it, and the serpent knew that, *As long as God doesn't show up at this moment, I've got her.*

She reached out her hand. Something strange was going on inside of her. It was as if two foes were battling each other in her mind. One entity tried to hold her back. The counterargument tried to convince her: *Grab it and take a bite. After all, it looks so good.* She felt as if a thousand hands were on her back, nudging her toward the fruit, yet there was only one to hold her back. Her conscience told her, *Run away.* But her eyes revealed a different tactic.

"Go ahead, go get it."

Her eyes urged her to continue.

"Besides, God isn't even here. How will He ever know?"

She was getting weaker.

"I will try just one bite and keep it to myself. What harm can it do?"

The serpent was smiling widely and resisting the desire to drool. He licked his lips to hide his bloodlust.

She held out her other hand and the deceiver gave it to her. She lifted it up to her nose and smelled it.

Oh, this is going to be so good, the devil said to himself. He was even leaning forward.

Both the woman and the serpent were filled with anticipation but for different expectations.

The world will soon be mine. These two will be gone. Everything is going according to plan. First I will get this woman to fall into disobedience, and then I will use her to get the man to follow. Like a large rock rolling down a hill, once the process has begun, there will be no stopping it. Satan mulled over each step of his scheme.

The woman stuck out her tongue and licked the outside of the fruit and smiled. Her eyes brightened, and then she sunk her teeth in deep and ripped off a piece. Instantly, a sinking sensation totally overwhelmed her. As she continued to chew, the feeling of carrying something heavy on her back grew larger. She chewed, and the feeling grew to the point of being a burden. And she swallowed it, and her eyes felt as if they had passed through a veil. Then she followed them through a dark tunnel. She got to the other side, and instantly, to her, the world looked different, darker, and colder.

At that moment, she heard a sound, an awful moaning sound that seemed to well up all around her. "Where is that noise coming from?" she asked the serpent. "Surely you heard it too."

"Uh, what noise?" Satan replied.

She took another bite, and the heaviness, as well as that sound, grew larger. She turned her eyes from the fruit and beheld the serpent laughing. "Why are you laughing? None of this seems funny at all."

She noticed that he was no longer so smooth and colorful but was sneering as he laughed at her, and there appeared to be horns protruding from his forehead. His outer flesh took on a rough, sharp, and scaly appearance.

They both heard the sound of the moan as it got louder, and they stared at each other.

Satan considered. "I've heard that sound before as I was judged and kicked out of heaven with one-third of all the angels, only to fall to this desperate location." He quickly summed up all the facts and realized what the source of the groaning was.

But the woman was confused. Gone was the pleasant vibration

that every living being emanated. Now there was a dull silence with barely a pulse. Still trying to determine the source of that awful groaning, she gazed upon the serpent once more. He now looked even more hideous to her, and the world took on an even darker hue.

CHAPTER SEVENTEEN

"I told you that I should not have eaten that fruit from that tree, I will never eat it again."

Her enemy replied, "What difference does that make to me? Go call your husband and give some to him. Wasn't it good?"

After she turned away to look for Adam, she thought within herself, *He was so excited to show me all around the garden and emphatic to show me those two trees. He had to show me that tree especially. Now I will show him that I've learned what he does not yet know. We will share this together as well and grow in wisdom together.*

The serpent told her, "Hurry and go find him. That fruit will stay fresh for only so long. You don't have much time."

It did seem to her, as if it was getting much warmer now. She even noticed that she was beginning to sweat. *Funny,* she thought. "Don't worry about this fruit going bad. I will just get him to come here with me and get his own piece to eat," she said.

The devil took note of that comment and realized his plan was working. *Now I have someone who can do my difficult work for me. She probably will have a much easier time getting him to partake than I ever could,* he thought to himself. But he cautioned her, "If he sees the piece you picked, with your bite mark in it, he will be much more likely to join you. He will never pick his own, since his Lord told him directly not to."

"So you think he will listen to me if God is not around and he sees that I already ate some?" she asked.

"That might be your best and only chance," the devil

suggested, thereby passing on the work of his plan to her.

"I will also emphasize to him that it is another good thing we need to share together." She then took the fruit and ran off, calling Adam's name.

These creatures, this world, will soon be mine, thought the serpent. *And oh how easy it will be to use them to do my bidding.*

It wasn't long before the woman ran into Adam. He was already on his way toward the spot where the trees were and had almost arrived before she ran to find him.

Instantly, he knew something was different. She didn't seem to have the same aura about her and seemed to be rough in her communication. He also wondered what that awful groaning sound or voice was. "Do you hear it?" he asked.

"Uh, what sound?" she replied.

Then he saw what she had in her hand. "Where did you get that?" he asked.

"Oh you won't believe what just happened. It's wonderful. That's why I was running to find you. Over there, by the tree. Quick, let's go."

Reluctantly, he let her pull him by the hand until they got to where the serpent had been.

"Where did he go?" She didn't know that he was still there, concealed in the underbrush just watching and waiting.

After quite some time and a lot of persuasion the woman was beginning to get Adam to succumb to her requests. She asked, begged, cried, pleaded, and made luscious promises that she knew would appeal to him and weaken his resolve.

That old serpent kept watching. He was totally glued to the drama that was unfolding before him. It was going too well. *I have made an incredible ally in this new helpmate of Adam's*, he began to think. *Clearly he is teetering and about to go down for the count.* Satan's mouth again began to water, and he uttered a quiet growl.

As Adam wavered, he decided not to summon any resolve to resist or to muster up the sense of responsibility within him that had caused him to turn the garden into a paradise. He put the image of his Friend's face out of his mind as soon as it appeared. "I didn't even consider my Maker's love or call to mind His words," he would later admit. Instead, he began to think about his wife. *I don't want to be separated from her. If she has found a new wisdom and wants to share with me, well, what's wrong with that? It will only make our unity stronger*, he lied to himself.

He looked at her. *She certainly isn't dead*, he reasoned. *And although she looks different than she did before I left for work, the difference is only slight. I just want to please her and make her happy. I have to do it!*

Adam took the fruit from her hand, and he also sunk his teeth into it.

Instantly, they noticed serious changes. These were drastic in comparison to the subtle changes that had occurred after she alone had eaten the fruit.

That groaning sound seemed to be coming from everywhere. It was all around them, and they could even feel it. Adam looked at her and said, "I think all of creation is crying."

Adam felt a strong sense of heaviness come upon him, and his inner joy was getting choked out and turning to suspicion. When he looked into the sky and around him, he no longer felt a sense of wonder but dread. Then Adam looked at her and recoiled at her nakedness. He realized that they were both naked and felt an overwhelming urge to run and seek cover. He looked at her again and felt blame. Adam was also angry with her and resented his wife for the first time. He began to argue with her right there in the presence of the deceiver, and she felt the need to deflect all of his accusations onto the serpent, had who lied to her.

"And who are you to put this all on me anyway? I didn't make you eat anything. You did that part all by himself," she claimed.

He felt very vulnerable and grabbed her by the hand and said, "Let's go."

They ran together deep into the woods and hid behind a cluster of leaves.

The woman began trailing behind Adam and said, "I am feeling certain that nobody can see us now."

Every now and then, they would hear an unfamiliar sound and get very apprehensive. "What was that? Did you hear that? Get down. Someone is coming. You're going to get us caught," he hissed.

Adam saw a mother bear attack and chase off a full-grown male that was stalking her cubs. "Did you see that?" he asked. "I have never seen them act so strangely before."

Then he yelled out in pain and again accused his wife for this too.

"What are you talking about?" she asked.

"You stuck something sharp in my arm."

"No I didn't," she retorted.

When they looked at where his arm hurt, they saw a wound and had to pull out a six-inch long thorn. "Where did that come from?" they both asked at the same time, in wonder.

I must have run my arm against this branch when I was waving off the cubs to try to save them, he figured.

"Wow, how did it get so long? Watch out! There are so many of those long thorns all around us. What is going on?" he said.

As they were whispering to each other, he put his finger to his lips and said, "Shhh! Did you hear that?"

"Quit playing that silly game," the woman said to her husband. "There is no one there."

"I heard footsteps. We'd better go deeper to hide."

"I think I did hear that too. It sounds like it's getting closer. Stay down. Let's go," the woman urged.

The two went deeper and deeper into the forest. "What the heck? It wasn't this thick in here a few hours ago. It seems so much more difficult to move around. This was a well-kept forest floor. Look out. There are tangles of vines and prickly things growing up all around," he cautioned. "We will have to pull them out of our skin later. But right now, we need to quickly get away from those footsteps. I think it's the Lord. Maybe He is coming to kill us for eating from that tree," he added.

Instantly, they knew that He would know and that they had to cover up their nakedness.

CHAPTER EIGHTEEN

The Father was there early, like He was every morning. This was where they met every morning. But now Adam and his wife were not there like they always were. The trees and bushes all looked different. They looked wild. The Father sat down upon a low-lying branch and waited.

When it became uncomfortably well past their usual meeting time, He began to call his name. "Adam. Adam? Adam, where are you."

He waited to see if he could hear any response, anything. There was nothing.

When He got up to look around, He felt a flush come over Him, and a sense of sorrow approached as if to taunt Him. He saw a half-eaten fruit from the tree of the knowledge of good and evil on the ground, and instantly He felt nauseous. He began to call out again, this time frantically and with anguish in His voice. "Adam, where are you?"

He cried long and loud but still there was no answer.

The longer He called for them, the more uncomfortable the man and his wife became. "That is Him. What should we do? He has come to kill us," the woman said to her husband. "You said He told you that, on the day that you eat of that tree, you will die the death. He must mean that He will kill us as our punishment for disobeying Him."

"No, that can't be it," Adam said. "He would never kill us. We were friends. If He keeps calling me, I am going to go. He will find us eventually anyway. If we go now, maybe He won't be so angry over what we did—if He doesn't have to come and keep looking to find us."

"How will He know what we did? Just don't tell Him," suggested the woman.

"Believe me, He knows. He knows already. He probably knew we would do it when He first told me not to, and since He has been calling for so long He might have figured it out."

This conversation kept the two frozen in place.

The Almighty kept calling. Finally it became clear to them that He was not going to leave. Adam and his wife looked at each other with ashen faces. Terrified, he spoke first, "I am going to Him. You come behind me."

Then both got up, wrapped themselves in a tangle of fig leaves, and walked the distance. They stepped out into the pathway, and as they approached Him, they knew that He knew that something was wrong. They could see grief-stricken sorrow over His whole being. He was not beaming with joy this time, unlike every other time upon their arrival for their daily fellowship. Rather, He was pensive as if He knew what must be done but did not enjoy the thought of having to do it.

Nevertheless, He told Himself, *I am going to question them and hear them out.* The righteous judge of all creation was going to give the presumed guilty their opportunity to represent themselves before Him.

Adam and his wife were shaking with fear, uncertain if death was coming for them from His swift, powerful hands.

"Where were you?" He asked.

"I was naked, so I hid," came Adam's reply.

"Who told you that you are naked?" came the response. "Have you eaten from the tree that I told you not to eat from?"

Then Adam, feeling that he could pin the whole thing on Him replied, "The woman who You gave to be with me, she gave me the fruit from the tree, and I ate some."

Then the Judge squared His gaze at the woman and said, "Why have you done this?"

The woman attempted to cast blame on the serpent. "The serpent tricked me, and I ate some," she said.

The last one to stand before the Righteous Judge, again, was that old serpent.

At that moment Adam and his wife both knew that this would not be the last time the One would judge the other.

"Because you have done this, you are now cursed above all animals. From now on, you will crawl on your belly everywhere you go and eat dust as you go, all the days of your life," He continued. "I will put hatred between your seed and her Seed. He will crush your head, and you will bruise his heel."

Then He looked again at the woman and said, "I will greatly increase your childbearing pain. In anguish, you will bring forth children, and your desires will be subjected to your husband."

Turning His gaze one more time upon Adam, He said, "Because you obeyed the wishes of your wife and disobeyed Me by eating from that forbidden tree, cursed is the ground for your sake. In sorrow and toil will you cultivate food from the soil for the rest of your life. Thorns and thistles will proliferate where you toil. Your work will become much harder, and through sweat and painful labor will you produce your bread until you return to the dust from which you came."

God's work was not finished yet. The next decisive action that he took was not as the judge but instead as the redeemer. He took an innocent lamb and cut its throat right in front of them. They watched and gasped as God held the lamb up on a tree while the blood drained from his neck all over the ground. Blood came out so fast that some of it splattered up onto the man and his wife from head to toe. They just stood there and accepted it as part of the consequence for their sin. They knew the lamb had been slain for them—in their place. The Father then took the lamb's skin and made garments for Adam and his wife to cover their nakedness.

The Lord said in conference, "Now that man has become like Us in knowing good and evil, We must remove them from the garden where the tree of life grows in order to keep them from taking the fruit of it and living forever."

While Adam and his wife were still reeling from what they had just experienced, they were sent forth out of the garden of Eden by God—forever. He too was going to leave the garden and never return to it again. He was no longer going to meet with Adam as a friend meets his friend. Whether or not Adam was going to see God on earth again, he was too scared to ask. They were banished and told to work the ground outside for their living.

After the two former occupants were physically evicted, the Judge posted a strong angel to guard the entrance of the garden from every direction in order to protect the tree of life. "In time, that beautiful place will become obscured into the landscape by neglect and ignorance," God concluded.

Prior to his departure, the Father prophesied the truths to Adam and his wife—telling them what would transpire. He spoke of the One to come, the Seed, born of a woman to redeem the dead unto everlasting life.

He continued, "All things must become new. Finished are the mornings when I can walk through the garden with Adam, the apple of My eye. Gone are the days when you gain and maintain order through your work in the earth. In place of order will be a never-ceasing battle with decay and chaos and encroaching erosion and the aging march of nature toward the day when the earth wears out like a garment.

"Your relationship with Me will be forever different. No longer will it be open and face-to-face as before. But from now on, you will receive revelation of God and of your eternal need. The culmination of all the revelations through the years will result in the advent of the Seed. Man's situation is very serious now, and his need is great. Yet no one can do anything about it. Only by the mercy of God can man's condition and need be both satisfied and ameliorated. Death has stepped onto the scene, and it will claim as its victims not only you two living souls who took part in that day's drama but also all of creation and all future offspring until the Seed of the woman shouts His victory cry over death. In that day, He will lead captivity captive and swallow death up in the victory of life. He will say to death, 'Where is your sting?'"

Then He departed from them for the last time.

CHAPTER NINETEEN

Nobody thought much about the serpent after the fallout from the eviction of Adam and his wife from the garden. They just assumed that he had slithered off into the bushes never to be seen or heard from again. Unfortunately, Satan wasn't that simple. He was just in the beginning phases of implementing his own plan. "The husband and wife never see me anymore but I am still here, watching, listening and waiting," he told his followers.

"Be fruitful and multiply," Adam whispered. "That is what He said to us. Perhaps through our offspring, all things can be made right again. Your seed will bring back joy and the presence of the Lord."

Satan heard them say that and laughed.

That night the woman conceived. And in the fullness of nine months, she gave birth to a son. Again, a name had to be given. Adam then gave his wife the name Eve because "you are the mother of the living." Then he named his son Cain.

In the process of time, Adam and Eve had many children. Sons and daughters were born to them. One little boy, whom they named Abel, seemed different from his brothers and sisters. His mother, Eve, wondered, *Could this be the one who is to come and will deliver us?*

As they grew up, Cain and Abel chose farming as their profession. Cain became very skillful at bringing the crop to harvest. Adam thought, *He reminds me of myself back when I was in the garden of Eden.* Cain could take a wild, infertile piece of

94

land and, through perseverance and application of the skills Adam had taught him, make it quite productive. Through his work, the effects of the curse seemed to have diminished. He noted, "There is such a difference between the ground now compared to how it produced before the incident with the fruit and the tree." *Could he be the one we have waited for?* Adam wondered. *Our food is plentiful and varied thanks to Cain.*

Adam and Eve and all their children had never eaten so well before. The thorns and the perspiration were set at bay, and a victory over these afflictions, seemed to have been secured. They asked each other, "Could this be the crushing of the serpent's head?"

Abel, on the other hand, chose to work with livestock. "Like his father before him," Adam bragged, "he has a way with animals. He also has a uniqueness to him. He seems quiet and attentive to the unseen entities, as if even aware of a presence that no one else can see." Adam had since given up on the hope of ever meeting face-to-face with God again. "He never returned to walk with me after the sentencing," Adam told his family. "We no longer have open access to God's presence."

Could Abel be the one who would tear down the wall and bring them into open fellowship again? he privately hoped.

Cain and Abel worked day after day in the fields. Adam gradually relinquished the responsibility of providing with his hands to them. He took on more of an advisory role. In the midst of his life, under the curse, he could see the mercy, goodness, and blessing of God being given to them all. The two brothers spent countless hours working together and becoming like two prongs of a pitchfork. Their siblings even nicknamed them "the field-to-food crew."

It was all going so well. Yet, again, they were being watched. Adam thought, *It has been a long time since I repressed that painful memory of that conflict with the serpent and my Maker. It has also been too long since I reminded my children to always stay true to the commandments. I must make a resolution to myself to do better that way.* He only thought about how the two brothers worked well together in the fields and that they could accomplish any job they set out to do. He never considered that they were not prepared for a spiritual struggle that would require their cooperation.

Silently, patiently waiting, their unknown enemy, the deceiver, grew increasingly agitated with how well this happy family was prospering. "I can't stand for this," Satan told his newest helper, Anarchy. "If things keep going this well, some of these people will never fall. This is my new challenge. My consuming purpose is to slay them." Like a lion stalking his prey, the devil studied the family of Adam and Eve, looking for any sign of weakness, any opening.

It was looking to be a very busy day on the farm. Everyone in the family who had not moved away had much to do. Nevertheless, this was a day to make a sacrifice. Adam insisted that the two leaders wait before leaving so they could perform their duty to God before going way out into the field. The brothers, on the other hand, had a different idea, which they explained to their father, hoping to blend work with obligation. Ultimately, they were attempting to persuade him into allowing them to make time for their sacrifice during their long work break. The two brothers looked at each other, and Abel knew it was his job to assure his dad that they wouldn't overlook this sacred duty. Since it was him who gave the assurance, Adam relented.

Prior to leaving their father's presence, the brothers decided that they would take their long break in the evening and perform their sacrifice at that time. Abel was anticipating the ceremony. He had a male lamb tied up for the event. It was a beautiful yearling and had not a single mark on it. He even named it the lamb of

God. "With this offering, I know God will be pleased," he said. And he talked about it all day long as they worked together in the field.

"Are you trying to be annoying? Must you keep talking about your sacrifice being the lamb of God? You are really beginning to get on my nerves," Cain said. As Cain's work began to tire him out, he was getting even more agitated and didn't realize how angry he was.

Satan was watching. He understood what was happening. "I have an opportunity here. I will seize upon this opportunity," the deceiver said.

He jumped right in to Cain's thoughts and fired up an unknown animosity toward his brother and even the whole sacrifice.

He's always trying to look better than me, came the thought, *always doing things to look like the hero.*

As the day progressed, Cain continued to listen to Abel, who became increasingly excited about his devotion and duty, and to those thoughts.

Almost like music from his instruments, Abel would describe how, "worthy the God is for Whom he would give his best." He would say things like, "I am certain that God will accept this perfect sacrifice. That is exactly what He requires." And then he began to talk about being, "one with God."

Cain yelled angrily, "I can't take it anymore."

At that point, Cain broke and yelled out in rage at Abel, "Knock it off and just shut up. He said that what they had to do was not such a big deal to him and that he was tired of hearing about it, concluding, "God will be fine with whatever either of us offer."

As far as I'm concerned that little lamb is not sufficient for the job in comparison to all the produce from the field that I heaped up as my sacrifice, Satan whispered.

Cain listened to that idea. *That's right*, he agreed and went further, muttering, "But I am not going to brag about it all day long."

Envy responded to Satan's call and immediately arrived with more suggestions for Cain. "Actually, by now anyone would be incensed by his annoying actions," mumbled Cain, right along with the planted thought. He got pretty spiteful about the differences between their two choices and insisted, "No innocent one's death could take the place of the guilty."

Satan explained to Cain, *Abel has to pay for his own sin with his own cost, just like you are going to do, or it will be Abel who will be left out of God's acceptance.*

Abel simply replied, "If that was true, brother, then God would not have taken our parents fig leaves from them and provided a covering from the innocent lamb that was slain for them."

Cain replied, "It doesn't matter." He added that, in his opinion, they should perform their duties separately and not together.

Abel sadly answered, "If you think it is best, brother."

Cain went off into the distance with his wagonload of produce to erect an altar and sacrifice alone.

Although the brothers set up their altars with a vast distance between them, the gap was not too big for the presence of God to be at both. Satan was there too but only with Cain.

After Abel tied the lamb onto the altar, he slit the throat of the innocent sacrifice that had been chosen. He received greater insight into what was actually happening. A still small voice spoke to him. Though the words not audible, they were clear and unmistakable: *This is very pleasing to Me, Abel. The blood of this innocent sacrifice serves to cover your sins. You have done well to select a perfect lamb and sacrifice that which I require. Enter into the fellowship with the Almighty One, Who loves you.*

Abel continued to worship. His vocal offering of joy and acceptance could be heard in the distance by Cain.

Cain was almost set and ready with his offering when he heard it again. "That voice!" he said. Satan kept whispering to him and it was driving Cain mad.

"He is so irritating," Satan continued. "All he talked about all day was his little lamb. He called it the lamb of God and went on and on about how much joy it gives him. Now you can't even get your thoughts straight to focus on what you gotta do because of his incessant singing."

Cain picked up a rock and threw it in Abel's direction. "Shut up!" he yelled. But he knew he wouldn't be heard over Abel's loud singing.

As the sheaves of wheat and grain roasted on the fire, Cain felt as if somebody was talking to him. A little voice, Satan's, was telling him to "put more work into your sacrifice." Cain responded by dumping more and more of his produce from the field onto his altar. The flames went high up into the air as he piled them on, hoping his offering would do for him what Abel's had done for him. His brother's choice had such a pleasing effect. His didn't. Rather, Cain only grew depressed and angry at his futility.

"Keep trying," Satan whispered, trying to push him over the edge.

"Such a waste," he mumbled.

Just go over there and shut him up, he thought. But where had that idea come from?

He looked around him but didn't see anybody.

If you hit him with the next rock you throw, that will shut him up. Then you both can get back to work.

The Almighty Judge intervened into Cain's mind at that moment. *Why are you so angry? You know what is required. If you offer the right sacrifice, then you will be accepted.*

Be careful, Cain, He said. *Sin is crouching right at the door of your mind, and its desire is for you. Master it by choosing righteousness.*

"If God is not satisfied with what I have given today, that's too bad. Satan approved this idea. I am going over there to see Abel and let him know how disturbing he is," Cain said. As he covered the distance between them, Cain's anger only grew. As he got closer he came upon a hand-sized rock.

"Perfect," Satan said.

Cain picked it up as he closed the gap between he and Abel. After a short interaction, Abel turned away from him. Angry at this reaction, Cain realized that suddenly he was behind Abel. Without another thought, his hand came down hard on the back of Abel's head, rock in hand.

More blood. This time, it wasn't just the lamb's. As Abel's blood poured out, he slumped at his brother's feet, and his blood mixed with that of the "lamb of God" at the base of the altar. He exhaled one last large breath. He was dead.

ABOUT THE AUTHOR

Chris Pagano is married to Alyce, who has been his sweetheart since their youth, for twenty-nine years. Together, they have three awesome children—Hannah, 23; Guytano, 20; and Duncan, 17. They live in St. Clairsville, Ohio. Chris is an alumnus of Regent University in Virginia Beach, where he graduated with a master's degree in education. He has been working in the public school system for twenty-four years.

Chris owns several residential properties that he manages and/or restores for future sale. He enjoys coaching his sons in basketball, currently as the coach of his youngest son's high school basketball team.

Chris hopes to publish the sequel to *So Shall It Forever Be* within the coming year. Please visit his website to let him know how this book has affected you.

It is his hope that, after reading *So Shall It Forever Be*, you will go back to the original source of the story in the Bible and search for the truths hidden there regarding these things.